MW01173290

When God Says NO

Crossing The Bridge From Pain to Purpose

By

Elaine M Prioleau

Copyright © 2021 Elaine M. Prioleau

All rights reserved. No part of this publication may be reproduced, distributed, or transmitted in any form or by any means, including photocopying, recording, or other electronic or mechanical methods, without the prior written permission of the publisher, except in the case of a brief quotations embodied in critical reviews and certain other noncommercial uses permitted by copyright law.

Although every precaution has been taken to verify the accuracy of the information contained herein, the author and publisher assume no responsibility for any errors or omission. No liability is assumed for damages that may result from the use of information contained within.

Printed in the United States of America. First printing: March 2021

ISBN: 9798721133848

DEDICATION

This book is dedicated to my parents, Rev. Dr. John Bee Moore and Rebecca Moore, who found enough room in their hearts to love a child who was left to be unloved. Thank you to my husband, James, who continues to be "my rock." Thank you for standing and remaining strong, listening to me, and being my sounding board. Thank you for seeing me at my worse and still loving me unconditionally. Thank you to my kids, who never stopped believing in me, encouraging me, and loving me. God entrusted His most precious gifts to me, and you have given me more than you know. I pray I will continue to grow into the mother God sent me to be for you. To my grandchildren, Nya, DeRaylen, Chris Jr., and Raydrian, you all have shown me and given me a love that cannot be compared. Being your Grandma, Nana, and MeMa are titles I don't take for granted, and I feel privileged to even have them bestowed upon me. I only pray I will live up to your godly expectations of me. To my crew, my eating partners, prayer partners, and cut-up crew, The Bonnet Ministry, thank you. Your nuggets of knowledge, encouragement, and prayers helped make this possible. Special thanks to "The Bishop" and "The Prophet," who poured into me and helped me give birth to my "baby." Thanks to Wanda Roberts who took me under her "writing wings" and taught me how to transcribe thought to paper. Thanks to Toccara Steele who from the day we has pushed, pulled and tugged all the way from Chicago. And to every person who endured my transitions and never walked away, I am forever grateful. It is my prayer you will receive continued unmerited grace and favor.

When God Says No: Crossing the Bridge from Pain to Purpose

TABLE OF CONTENT

INTRODUCTION

I don't like heights. I have an immense fear of being up high, so I don't ride roller coasters and have only begun to *somewhat* enjoy flying. My greatest fear is bridges, especially bridges over water. In my mind, bridges don't offer the proper support I think is necessary. How is that? Bridges have columns to hold them up, but they are still elevated above land and water, and in my mind, that's a problem. That's not enough. There is still an expanse between me and the bottom, the ground, or the water. What's worse than a bridge is a long bridge. Long bridges combined with fear can make us doubtful and paralyzed. I know to get to certain places, I will have to cross bridges, whether they are long or short, high, or low. If I want to get to my determined destination, I will have to cross bridges. I realized I will have to face whatever comes, regardless of how painful it is, how fearful I get, what I gain, or what I lose. One thing I have learned is eventually, the bridge will come to an end if I keep going. I have heard the quote so often before, *it's not the destination as much as it is the journey*. But what if the journey is filled with missing pieces, twists, and turns? What if the bridges we are crossing keeps getting higher and higher? What if the journey turns out to be what we feel is the most horrible experience ever? How do we handle getting from one side to the other without falling through the cracks or missing planks? What do you do when you want to go in one direction, and the one you have trusted to direct you says no, take this route, and that route is filled with hurt, pain, and disappointment? How do you get to the other side when it feels like your lifeline has run short, and the SOS signals for help have failed? Will you make it to the other side, you ask? I want you to know that, YES! YES, YOU WILL!

We all have had times in our lives when we desired something or someone intensely. We have experienced the excitement of having our desires coming to fruition and watching our dreams come to life. There is something about having the very thing you desire right there at your fingertips. Then there have been those times when something was so close, you could taste it—the sweet smell of victory, the arrival of all you have ever hoped for, the end of your metaphoric rainbow, the cherry to your sundae. I have experienced many times a desire so intense, I could not eat or sleep. It consumed me to the point, I thought I would die without it! I was such a fool. I look back and shake my head in disbelief.

This book is not about one incident or one desire. It is not about any one person or relationship, but in the spirit of transparency, it comes from a place of experience, relationships, situations, people… life.

For whatever reason you picked up this book and are reading it, it seems safe to say you, too, have faced various situations on your own that have been difficult to navigate. So, as you read this, my hope is this will be a tool you, like me, will find helpful and enable you to get through some of the turbulent times in your life. As you cross the various bridges in your life, from wherever you are to your designated purpose—and yes, you have purpose, which has already been designated for you—I pray this will help you get through that heartbreak, denial, dismay, upset, setback, set up, let down, roadblock, whatever you may call it when the very thing you hoped for or desired doesn't manifest the way you thought. This is for those, like me, who have sought God for the answers to all the things in your life you felt you wanted, needed, desired, felt entitled to, and for whatever reason, have felt as though your prayers were unanswered. This is for those of us who have cried tears of frustration and had questions only God could answer. When we have prayed and prayed about something, and that prayer seems to fall on deaf ears, there's a certain pain, or discomfort one feels when it seems as though they've been denied by God, almost a feeling of betrayal. Now mind you, I can only speak for myself. This is my point of view, but I know until I began to understand the "is-ness" of God, I thought all the things I was doing "for God" would exempt me from any more disappointment or trouble. I thought that finally deciding the path I needed to take would ensure the very things my heart desired would be granted. News flash—it did the very opposite. Aligning myself with God's will put me in a place to be disappointed and hurt because it meant I would have to deny my flesh and its selfish desires, and that was and is hard. Aligning myself also ensures I have the peace in my life I so greatly need, the joy I so desperately need, and the satisfaction of knowing not only is my relationship with God elevated, but God loves me so intently, so deeply, so fully, so recklessly, He is anti-anything that is anti-me. If it means I hurt for a moment to receive what He has for my destiny and eternity, that is a chance I am willing to take and a sacrifice I'm willing to make.

The steps in this book are not things I came up with just for fun. These are actual things I experienced, went through, and techniques tried and true that helped me understand the importance of God's will in my life. These steps also helped me to mature in my relationship with God. They do not have to be done in a certain order. Everyone's situation is different and will have to be dealt with in the manner that fits them. I have gone through these steps, and as I am writing this, I am going through one or two of these steps. Why? Because we are never at a point in our lives that we are not coming to a bridge, crossing a bridge, on a bridge, or getting ready to come off of a bridge. This book has caused some things to arise in my life I thought I had dealt with, so I am having to search myself and see where I am on this bridge and how do I get across? So, I encourage you to not only read this book but to take a moment to reflect and self-examine yourself. Read the questions and be transparent with yourself. Each section is designed, so you can take notes, write your prayers, doodle, or whatever makes you feel comfortable. Perhaps you do not know what to write. That is okay. God already knows what you're feeling and dealing with, so you don't have to attempt to hide your true thoughts from Him. I pray this will also serve as a tool that will help you cross the bridge from where you are to where it is God wants to take you, and that as you cross the bridge, step by step, crying and maybe fearful and frustrated, you will hold God's hand and let Him lead you.

Chapter 1

DID YOU REALLY JUST TELL ME NO?!

So, let me go on and make you upset, and for those who would like to argue this next statement, go ahead. From my personal experience, it is my belief God does not always give you whatever you ask for. I don't care how much you cry, beg, or bargain with Him, He's not going to always give you whatever you ask for. Why not, you ask? I'm glad you did. He is not going to readily give you anything that goes against His word, as simple as that. That's the catch. If whatever we think we want or desire is causing us to behave, act, think, or do what is contrary to what His Word has said, there's no point in even asking. That doesn't mean we can't act upon our desires to gain what we want, but you must understand will. God's will for our lives is greater than what we can imagine. For us to have and live in abundance, we must let God be God. It's when we assert our will, the problem comes in, and because we're human, we do what we do. We ask. We see it, feel it, think it, desire it, then we ask. I often wonder what goes through the mind of God when we're thinking things.

I remember growing up and wanting to go out to parties and dances. I would muster up the courage to ask my mother and would preface it with, "There's a dance after the game on Friday," and before I could even finish the sentence, she would say, "If you even think you're going, there's no need to even ask because the answer is no." Mind you, my parents were the strictest in the world. I have people to verify that, but I won't mention names. What they were trying to do was to keep me from what they perceived was wrong, dangerous, or just downright harmful in some instances. In some cases, I was going to engage in things I shouldn't have, but that's for another book. My parents believed by telling me no, they were doing what was best for me. There were times I would continue to ask, but not for long. My mother had this thing that if you kept asking, you'd really be in trouble. What they also were doing was preparing for me for a time in my life I wouldn't be able to get everything I wanted, and I needed to be able to handle being told "no." Sadly, I see a generation of people who have made life-changing decisions because of their inability to handle and process being told "no." In order to build character and integrity, we must be able to receive denial and pray we can then be open to see the denial was not in an attempt to withhold things we find desirable but could be saving us from possible detrimental consequences.

I remember one occasion, I really wanted to do something, and my parents finally gave in. I wanted to participate in a talent program for school instead of the fundraiser for the church. I asked over and over until they finally agreed. "What will your talent be" they asked, and I told them ever so boldly, I was going to dance. They should have laughed in my face and forced me to do the fundraiser for church. First, everyone knows I CANNOT dance. Second, I was choosing a secular activity over an activity that would benefit the church and God's ministry. As a Southern Baptist, hell-fire-and-brimstone pastor, my dad was not pleased. Mostly, everyone knows I CANNOT dance. Well, instead of continuously saying no, they said yes. Let's just say, until this day, that was one of my most memorable and humiliating times in high school. I don't blame them. Their first response of "no" was not an effort to keep me from enjoying myself, but because they were wise enough to know it wasn't going to turn out well for me. After it was over and I had duly embarrassed myself, they helped me see everything I thought I wanted or needed wasn't always in my best interest. That memory still lingers in my mind, and I still feel embarrassed about it at times and laugh at myself. Why did I ever think I could be Janet Jackson?! Even now when I hear "Control," I think back and laugh.

But know this, God is not going to give you the green light to go wrong, do wrong, or willingly allow you to make the wrong choices.

That's just not going to happen. If you ask him to give you the go-ahead to do wrong, be prepared for Him to say no. If what you desire to do will cause you danger, He's going to say no. If what you're doing is not beneficial to yourself, others, or for His purpose and His glory, He will say no. Mind you, I keep saying, "He won't GIVE YOU the go-ahead to do wrong," but He WILL ALLOW you to make the decisions you want. When you say, "Did you really just tell me no? You don't want me to be happy, Lord," like my parents, He will loosen the reins and let you "go for yours." He will "let you be great." He will "let you do you." He will allow you to express "YOLO." And guess what? Even if the decision you make is one you shouldn't have made, He will be there, waiting with arms wide open to help you get brushed off, cleaned up, and back on track.

Being able to make the right decisions means we must eliminate all the options, distractions, and things that would cause us to lose focus of who God is. When God is trying to show us and lead us in a certain direction, it is important we recognize we can't be led if we are trying to be the leader. He can't lead if we're always jumping in the way with our own agenda or stipulations. Those things become blinders, and we're not able to see Him for who He is. It's not enough to just know Him as God who provides, heals, or answers prayers. He isn't just a God we can put our orders in and expect He will deliver. I often tell people, He's not a vendor machine God. We can't just put in our "coins" of sporadic prayer and worship and think when we press the button, what we want is going to fall out. To know if what we are doing is within the will of God and what He desires for us, we have to know Him as sovereign, Jehovah, Almighty Father, Prince of Peace, Lord of Lords, everlasting father, the one true and living God, the God who is high and lifted. Yes, that God! We must know Him to be omnipresent, omnipotent, and omniscient. We must know Him as immutable and a promise keeper. We must know Him as the one who already laid the plan out for our lives even before we were a thought. So, we can have all that it is, He gives us the directions we need. "Seek FIRST the kingdom of God and his righteousness and all these things will be added unto you." Matt 6:33 (NIV)

One thing I've learned is we must make a conscious decision to do what's right, to want God's will, and to experience His best. It's not by might or power but by God's spirit, His grace, and His mercy that will help us to elevate in Him. Sometimes, doing what's right is such a hard thing to do. Paul tells us, "I have discovered this principle of life, that when I want to do is right, I inevitably do what is wrong." Romans 7:18 (NLT) Now, isn't that something to be said? This is one of the greatest apostles to ever live, and even he was struggling. Just because we decide to follow Christ doesn't mean it's going to be smooth sailing—quite the contrary. Once we decide we are going to follow Christ, we have become Enemy #1 for the devil to try to destroy us. When we are doing all the things that make him happy, he has no reason to wage an attack on us, but as soon as we declare we are walking with Christ, we are no longer welcome to his party. And that's just fine with me. Going back to my story earlier about my parents—had they not downright and blatantly said no many times, I probably would have got in more trouble than I bargained for. It wasn't because I didn't want to be a good person. We all want to be "good people," but being a good person isn't enough in the eyes of God, which I think is difficult for us to accept sometimes. If we're good people, that should give us a one-up on those who aren't. One of the things I must be careful about is being ready to point out someone else's wrong and not addressing my own. The other thing I wrestle with is, just because I am walking more and more in the freedom of Christ, everyone else isn't there. So, for me to want them to own up to their wrong, so they can have the same freedom, it isn't for me to dictate. I must remind myself, against whose standards am I measuring myself by? Who am I comparing myself to who really has the capacity to determine my "goodness?" I've heard many people say, "Why is this happening to me? I'm a good person." Let's be honest. When people are sick, killed, or die unnecessarily, and we feel it's unfair, one of the first things people will say is, "Why did that have to happen? They were such a good person." This is seen quite often when people who live lifestyles that are not quite "squeaky clean," and their actions bring harm to others. Family members and friends will often say how good a person they were. While many believe their deaths are warranted, we must remember there is good in all of us, and we are not the one who gets to judge their eternal fate. While we all battle good and evil within ourselves, we must decide whether we will allow sin to dictate our actions. In our efforts to be a good person, who are we desiring to please? Who do we desire to follow and be like? We can easily get caught up in the cliché, "God knows my heart." And you know what? You're exactly right. God knows our hearts, so He knows that our hearts are filthy, dirty, broken, destroyed and in need of a total repair. To expand more on what Paul said in Romans 7:18-20 (NLT). "And I know that nothing good lives in me, that is, in my sinful nature. I want to do what is right, but I can't. I want to do what is good, but I don't. I don't want to do what is wrong, but I do it anyway. But if I do what I don't want to do, I am not really the one doing wrong; it is sin living in me that does it." And he was one of the most relevant men in the Bible. So, we see, there is none of us who are good; we are all sinners saved by grace. So often, we like to use that as an excuse to justify doing those things we shouldn't, so when we go to God in prayer, we will receive a favorable answer, but we have to pray as David prayed, "Create within me a clean heart and renew a right spirit within me." Psalm 51:10 (NASB) A clean heart helps us to be able to come to God with earnest prayers that desire His will over our own. In doing so, if God does say no, then we will have peace, knowing God is only doing what He knows is best. If I said you would always be happy, I would certainly not be truthful. You may not be happy in the sense of what the world considers happiness, but you would be able to find contentment in your life with God.

If we're not careful, we will develop an indignant attitude with God as though He is not allowed to have any say-so in our lives unless we allow Him to, and only if it's pleasing to us. Matthew 6:24 tells us, man cannot serve two masters, or he will love the one and hate the other. In this passage, he is addressing the issue of money, but in the same way it applies to money, it can also be applied to other areas of our lives. My father often used to say, "You can't straddle the fence." Either you are, or you're not. In Revelations, it speaks to us as being lukewarm, neither hot nor cold. We cannot go both ways. Either we're in with Christ, or we're out. If we choose to be in, we must be ALL the way in, with the understanding, sometimes on this journey, God is going to tell us things we don't want to hear and tell us to do things we don't want to do. He will allow some things to happen in our lives we're not going to like. The amazing and awesome thing about our God is, no matter what, He is going to be right there to walk with us and sometimes carry us through these unpleasantries in life. One of the worse feelings is to feel as though you are going through a storm all by yourself. Well, I want to encourage you—you are not alone!

It's funny, well not funny, but maybe you can say it was interesting or thought-provoking. I was once asked, "If you had a choice, who would you choose to follow? God or Satan?" Of course, as the good, saved, sanctified Christian I am, I quickly and boldly proclaimed, "God." My bubble was quickly burst when they replied, "If that's the case, why do you keep running after the enemy?" I dropped my head and cried. I cried out of sadness because the very thing I was desiring was the very thing that was taking me out of my character of God. I wanted so much for relationships to work, job offers to come, validation from others, apologies to be given, even at the expense of my own feelings and comfort, and at the expense of totally ignoring what God was trying to do in my life. I've wanted things to go my way. Even though I am a believer, even though I am a follower of Christ, even though I am worthy of love, even though I am not perfect and I am a "good person," I had to realize being a good person wasn't enough to keep me from wavering and following after something that was causing me to disregard everything I knew to not only be right but to be of God.

Let me interject this for those who may know me or know of my past. I am in no way perfect, nor am I the same person I used to be. I consider myself to be like the Apostle Paul when he said, "This is a trustworthy saying, and everyone should accept it—Christ Jesus came into the world to save sinners and I am the worst of them all." Because of certain situations in my life, I have come to a deeper understanding of who I am and *whose* I am. My past does not negate the call on my life by the Lord Jesus Christ. It allows me to be a vessel, so God can use me to speak to people's lives, people like me or you, who are wondering how to get to the place where they can look back and say, "God, it was nobody but you."

When I realized I was not going after God, the way I *claimed* to be, I cried. Once again, I felt I had failed God. (I'm told that I'm too hard on myself.) But let me interject before I go further—***I fell, but I didn't fail.*** I learned I could not fail or disappoint God. That would mean His existence and ability to be God was contingent on what I was able to do. I can't disappoint God because that would mean He is so dependent on me, He finds fault in me and convicts me. That is not of God. So, if you are one of those who feels they are such a disappointment and that their worth is dependent on other's approval of you, I encourage you to lift your head and know God loves you too much to be disappointed in you. He finds joy in you because you are His child.

I cried because that person was right. I was running after me because I didn't feel as though "no" was an acceptable answer. You know, sometimes, God will show you spiritual things, using very literal concepts that relate to everyday life. He showed me I was like a person on roller skates—very inexperienced, skating and chasing a dangling jewel. My legs were drifting farther and farther apart. I felt the sting and the pain, but I kept on skating and kept chasing. I felt the stretching, the increasing pain, and discomfort it was causing, but I kept chasing after the jewel. Now mind you, the jewel wasn't getting any closer. As a matter of fact, it seemed to get farther away, but I thought if I kept pushing to get it, eventually, it would be in my grasp. God showed me over and over how the jewel I was struggling to get was not what I needed. It was causing me too much pain, yet I continued to press. The more I chased the jewel, the less shiny and not as big as I thought it was. In fact, the closer I thought I was getting, the smaller it seemed. What was my way of pressing? Pleading, asking, begging, praying. Yes, I was praying for whatever I wanted so badly at that time, I was willing to risk everything—in some instances, even my life—to get it. And guess what God said? NO. Not just a calm, soothing no, but an adamant and emphatic NO. My response? Hey God, did you just tell me no?

"I fell, but I didn't fail."

Reflections

John 14:27

Peace, I leave with you; my peace, I give to you. Not as the world gives you do I give to you. Let not your hearts be troubled, neither let them be afraid.

Matt 11:28-30

Come to me, all who labor and are heavy laden, and I will give you rest. Take my yoke upon you, and learn from me, for I am gentle and lowly in heart, and you will find rest for your souls. For my yoke is easy and my burden is light.

Psalm 51:10

Create within me a clean heart and renew a right spirit within me.

Psalms 34:18

The Lord is near to the brokenhearted and saves the crushed in spirit.

Romans 7:18-20

And I know that nothing good lives in me, that is, in my sinful nature. I want to do what is right, but I can't. I want to do what is good, but I don't. I don't want to do what is wrong, but I do it anyway. But if I do what I don't want to do, I am not really the one doing wrong; it is sin living in me that does it.

Mark 10:18

So, Jesus said to him, "Why do you call Me good? No one is good but One, that is, God." (NKJV)

Write It Down

Be Honest About How You Feel

Part of starting this journey is being honest about how you feel. How do you feel when you feel as if He isn't giving you what you ask for? Or perhaps you received what you asked for and then were disappointed with your answer?

Write It Down

How You Feel Is Important

Sometimes, it feels as though God isn't listening when we pray. What do you do when you feel as though God isn't listening? How do you handle that?

Chapter 2

WHAT DO YOU MEAN NO?!

As Christians, I think we often feel we are exempt from hearing 'no' from God. Ok, well, maybe not you. I felt there were certain things I was exempt from. I knew soon, God was going to get tired of seeing me hurting, angry, broken, broke down, and broken hearted. I figured eventually, He would get tired of seeing me crying every single day, with headaches, and even with panic attacks and thoughts of suicide. You know, I had a job once I disliked so badly, I literally would get sick, knowing that I had to go in. If you would, let me interject something here. If you or someone you know is contemplating suicide, please seek help immediately. (insert 1800 number in the scriptures) Mental health issues are real. I pray God will surround you with the love, support, and help you need.

All my life, I had heard God wanted me to know happiness and peace, He would give you peace that passed all understanding, and He would not withhold any good thing from me. So, I knew He wanted me to be happy. Didn't He say he would give me joy and the desires of my heart? When we desire something strongly in our lives, that is the perfect opportunity for the enemy to come in and start planting seeds of deceit and trickery. He feeds us thoughts, trying to take the Word and use it against us. He loves to make us feel that God will not fulfill His promises to us. Much like the lies he told Eve in the Garden of Eden, he will try to get us thrown off track and to believe God is holding something back from us, but it's the very opposite. God loves us, but He doesn't always give us those things we ask for. The enemy likes to make us think everything we get that pleases us is a blessing. I like to look at them as "Trojan horses." If any of you are familiar with the story of the Trojan horse, you'll remember the Greeks, after ten years of unsuccessful attempts to defeat Troy, constructed a wooden horse to get inside the gates of their opponent. The city of Troy received the gift, but inside the horse were hundreds of soldiers hiding, who then jumped out, opened the gates to let in the Greeks into the city, and destroyed the city of Troy. That's how I envision the enemy when I am steadily trying to get or do things I know are against the will of God but satisfy my flesh. Normally, if your flesh is enjoying the situation to the point, it's starting to cause you to think ungodly or irrationally, then it's possibly not of God. The enemy loves to make you think you're getting a blessing, but in actuality, he is sending his imps, hiding inside the "Trojan horse," to destroy you with greed, lust, addiction, depression, oppression, ineffectiveness, laziness, unforgiveness… I think you got the picture. The thing I didn't tell you is all of those tears I cried, all the headache and heartache I endured, all the disappointments, anger, and abuse were only preparation for me to receive the even greater God had promised me. Getting to the point of seeing God in your situations and accepting His will in your life is a matter of time—year by year, month by month, week by week, day by day, minute by minute, second by second process—but it *is* possible. The scriptures tell us, "With man, it is impossible, but WITH Christ all things are possible." Mark 10:27 also tells us, "I can do all things through Christ Jesus, who strengthens me." Phil 4:13. So, it is God who does the work, we just must be the willing vessels.

So, back to the point of God not denying us any good thing. If what our heart desires is good, why would God tell us no, when we ask for it? God says in Psalms 84:11, "No good thing would He withhold from us." But it also says, "To those who do right." So, there are levels to this, and there is a requirement. For us to receive what God desires to give us, we must do what is right. What good things will He not withhold? He will not withhold peace, joy, wisdom, fulfillment, love, meekness, forgiveness, or everlasting life. Those are good things. No! Those are great things, and God desires we have those things, but if what we are striving to obtain takes away from His will and His purpose, He will not be inclined to give us what we are praying for. God hears and answers every prayer, but be prepared—the answer you get may not be the answer you want to hear.

Let's take a minute and look at Apostle Paul for a minute. In 2 Corinthians 12:7-10 when Paul says that he was given a thorn in his flesh, a messenger of Satan, an ungodly reminder, not to exalt himself. Three times he asked for God to remove the thorn and each time God said no. Why would a loving God not want to rescue Paul from this obvious pain, trial and obstacle? Didn't God care about Paul? Does God care about us? Of course, He did and He does. But let's look at what He tells Paul. He tells Paul, "My grace is sufficient for you, for power is perfected in weakness." Paul goes on to say that "I will rather boast about my weaknesses, so that the power of Christ may dwell in me. Therefore I am well content with weaknesses, with insults, with distresses, with persecutions, with difficulties, for Christ's sake; for when I am weak, then I am strong." So wait, you mean to tell me that the more issues I have, the stronger I am? How can that be possible? It's possible for us to be strong when God denies us our desires because it's in Him that we find our strength. It's in Him that we can dwell and it's through us that He can be glorified. When we are not given those things that readily bring us comfort or pleasure and we find ourselves growing closer to God, then God can do what it is He wants to do in our lives and He can be glorified. Our purpose for living is not to be missionaries and ministers, to be caregivers, parents, teachers, etc. Those are the vessels of position that are used to bring out the real purpose we are created for: to glorify God. When God does not do what we ask, it's not because He can't. Again it goes back to the will of God. When

God told Paul He would not remove the thorn, Paul didn't get upset and pout. But what he did was to push in closer to God and begin to boast of his weakness even moreso because it was in his weakness that God was able to show Himself as sustainer, provider, peace, joy, stability, sanity and whatever else Paul needed. And, God was able to carry out His purpose through Paul which was to minister to others to continue to bring them into the knowledge of Christ.

Let's go even deeper to a time when God did not grant the request of a prayer. When Jesus went to the garden of Gethsemane to pray, He prayed three times that "this cup would pass from me but not my will, thy will be done." He prayed three times that He would not have to give His life but each time He said not my will but thy will. And each time God did not respond but allowed His only son to give His life because He knew that losing His life would be the only way that we could have life. He had to allow Jesus to endure the cross so that the world then and to come would be able to be saved and have eternal life. So let's think about it. If God had to tell His own begotten son, "No" why do we feel that we should be exempt from being told no. We must learn to give God thank not just for the great things He has done. But, we have to be thankful for some of the things that He didn't do because His purpose in our lives must be fulfilled even if it means we are going to be uncomfortable.

Everything we consider to be good *to* us is not always good *for* us. There are a lot of things that cause us pleasure, we think are good or feel good. God will do His part to keep those things from us that will cause us harm, but He will also allow things to be if we are "bent" on having things our way. God did not create robots. He made us creatures of free will, and no matter how much power we think we have, we can't control what He ultimately decides to do and allow in our lives.

Reflections

Lamentations 3:22

The steadfast love of the Lord never ceases; his mercies never come to an end.

Deuteronomy 7:9

Know therefore that the Lord your God is God, the faithful God who keeps covenant and steadfast love with those who love him and keep his commandments to a thousand generations.

Matthew 7:8-11

For everyone who asks receive, and he who seeks finds, and to him who knocks it will be opened. Or what man is there among you who, when his son asks for a loaf, will give him a stone? Or if he asks for a fish, he will not give him a snake, will he? If you then, being evil, know how to give good gifts to your children, how much more will your Father who is in heaven give what is good to those who ask Him!

Joshua 21:45

Not one word of all the good promises that the Lord had made to the house of Israel had failed; all came to pass.

Hebrews 10:23

Let us hold fast the confession of our hope without wavering, for he who promised is faithful.

Write it Down

What Are You Praying For?

We have all prayed for things we really don't need or aren't what is best for us. What "good" thing(s) are you asking God for? Be honest with yourself. This is for your own reflection. What is your "why" for asking?

Write It Down

Is It Hurting/Helping?

Are the things you're asking for or praying about causing you to turn away from what you know God wants you to do?

Chapter 3

SCABS

So, now your feelings are hurt. You're angry, sad, and emotions are probably all over the place. Now what, you might ask? Which way and what's next? Well, before you go any further, let's talk about what's hurting. If you were like me, you ran, jumped ditches, played ball, and just ran carefree to your heart's content when you were little. I remember being a kid at my granddad's house. It was farmland, paths, trees, and ditches. One of the things we used to love to do was see if we could jump the ditch. It wasn't a huge ditch, but when you're a kid, it looks big and wide, and jumping it was a feat only the best could accomplish. I wasn't always sure if I would make it, and because of my fear, I often fell short of getting to the other side. There were times I fell and skinned my knees or my hands. If you played as roughly as I did, you probably injured yourself quite often. Well, at least I did. I was rather clumsy. Thankfully, I never broke a bone or seriously maimed myself. My mother was the type who would say, "Keep it up, you'll learn." Sure enough, I did, but it wasn't until after the expense of not listening. I endured my share of scrapes, cuts, bruises, and knots.

Growing up as a Pastor's kid, I was always at the church, doing whatever. I remember a time, one of my friends and I were running around downstairs in the annex area, playing while our parents were talking. Now, during this time, the floor was made from hard concrete, and there was a small stage with steps. My mother very plainly told me to stop running. Well, I fell and hit my head on the edge of the stage. I cried and cried and ended up with a huge cut on my forehead. Can you say painful? My mom put ice on it and after ensuring I hadn't severely injured myself or caused any brain damage, one of the first things that came out of her mouth was, "I told you to stop running! See what happens when you don't listen?" How often are we warned? How often does God attempt to divert our attention in a different direction to keep us from doing harm to ourselves or those connected to us, but we continue to run full speed ahead, injuring ourselves, crying, and needing him to help us?

How do bumps and scars help us? I cut my forehead and for years, had a small protrusion on my head. Even as I'm writing this, I'm rubbing my head and can still slightly feel the area where I hurt myself, but mostly, it reminds me of that day and experience. Now, unlike my mother, God doesn't ridicule us when we fall. He uses our scars to lead us back to Him. He uses the very thing He has allowed to bring us pain and allow us to see our dependence on Him and our need to have Him in our lives. He also uses those injuries and scabs as a way to show us, regardless of whatever may be going on in our lives, He is ever present. He will not chide or scold us, but even more than a loving parent, He stands with arms open wide.

The thing about being injured is at first, injuries don't always happen in the same manner, second, injuries don't always heal in the same amount of time, and third, injuries usually serve as a reminder to be careful and not do again what we did to become injured in that way. However, what is usually consistent with most injuries are scabs. Scabs are formed when platelets stick together like glue at the cut or injury. As the skin starts to heal, it gets hard and dries out, and a scab forms. Scabs are usually crusty and dark red or brown. The job of the scab is to protect the cut or injury by keeping germs and other impurities out and giving the skin cells underneath a chance to heal. I'm sure many of you reading this are not like me, you probably weren't impatient and inquisitive, but for those of you like me, you probably picked your share of scabs, instead of allowing them to fall off naturally. For some reason, I found scabs to be interesting. Who knows why?

So, scabs are part of the healing process but also serve as a form of protection. From what, you may ask? I'm glad you did. Scabs protect you from dirt, water, infection, and foreign objects. The hardness of the scab serves as a shield. The covering is not only formed to keep out things that could cause you more pain but also served as a covering of those things at work in your body to help you heal.

What a revelation!

When God says no, it can feel like an actual injury. Why? Whatever is tied to us—our desires, our dreams, our wants—can cause us to feel emotional and physical anguish. I'm going to be honest. When I was told no and finally accepted it... Wow! I felt as though my heart had literally been cut with a knife. It was worse when I fell and skinned the palm of my hand. The skin on the palm of your hand is thin, so when I fell, the rocks tore through my skin like paper. The pain was excruciating, and the healing process was painful, tedious, and one of the most uncomfortable feelings. My skin was rough, hard, ugly, and nasty. It itched, and all I wanted to do was to take the scab off, but taking the scab off before it was ready to come off would only have impeded the healing process.

When God told me the very thing my heart desired was not for me to have or told me it wasn't time to move or time to quit, or told me to ask for forgiveness to the very person who had hurt me, when God said, "not my will but His will," I can't even begin to describe the pain. That denial ripped through the thin skin of my emotions and at the very core of my soul. When the healing process began, it was rough, hard, and nasty. There was no medicine I could put on it, no way to blow it so it wouldn't burn, no Band-Aid large enough to cover what I felt was an unbearable wound. There was no bandage to stop the hypothetical bleeding. Listen, there were times God's denial or delay upset me so much, I figured there was no way

I could possibly go on.

As days passed, a scab began to form, and I began the slow and tedious healing process, then guess what? I snatched the scab off! Crazy, right? I didn't want to be reminded I had been hurt, that I had attributed to my pain. I didn't want to be reminded I had fallen once again. I didn't want to see I had fallen... again. The pride in me didn't want others to see I had failed by their standards. *But remember, I said I fell, but I didn't fail.* If you don't remember anything else from this book, remember, God never fails.

So, right then, the removal of my scab ceased to do what it was created to do. The scab that had formed over my heart to keep out the germs and dirt of anger, hurt, and unforgiveness began to seep in, and infection began to spread, all because I didn't allow proper healing to take place. Isn't it comforting to know, even when those things start to seep into our lives, they don't have to remain? They don't have to stay in our lives forever. With the proper treatment, they can be removed. We can be washed, cleansed, and made whole again. We can be healed, and our spiritual health be restored. Moving prematurely in our lives can cause us to have to start over, which can prolong the time as we know it, but just know, we will reach our planned destination at the God-appointed time. Yes, our destination is already planned.

One of my favorite scriptures now is Jeremiah 1:5. "Before I formed you in the womb I knew you, before you were born I set you apart; I appointed you as a prophet to the nations." God already has our life planned out, but we sometimes make choices that will take us down unpleasant paths God didn't intend for us to go. That doesn't mean we won't get where we are supposed to be. We won't be late or early—we will get there at the exact time we are supposed to. Just as He has planned out our lives, He is also aware of the paths we will take and has taken all that into consideration when putting our lives together. So, please don't think anything you have done, are doing, or will do is a surprise to Him. You don't have an inside scoop on your life, and you will never get a "one-up" on God.

Just as with physical injuries, God begins to form another scab over our brokenness to begin the healing process again. Even as I'm writing this, I'm not ashamed to say, there are still some areas in my life that have scabs. There are a lot of deep-rooted issues I have tucked away in the very corners of my heart and mind. These are scabs. There are injuries that are still in the process of or in need of healing. Why do I have scabs? Because I'm not perfect, because as I like to say, "I've done some jacked-up stuff in my life."

I'm willing to bet, though, if you look close enough, you will find a scab or two or three in your life. We are humans, imperfect and flawed creatures, so there is always a place in our lives that needs healing. Some of those scabs haven't yet fallen off on their own because we are not totally healed. We may still be holding on to guilt or regret. Perhaps we have not yet got over something that happened in high school, or perhaps our parents told us we would never be anything, or maybe we have been abused and haven't got over that hurt or the trauma of being violated. There is an area in all our lives that needs healing. Whatever you may find yourself still holding on to, let me reassure you, no matter what it is or who hurt you, even if you were the one hurting you, God loves you.

When he looks at you, he doesn't see your flaws, He sees his precious and beautiful child, his creation, his Masterpiece. His piece of creation He formed and mastered to His liking. If it's any consolation, He already knew we were going to mess up. He knows our propensities and intentions. As I said, nothing we have done has been a surprise to Him. So, if He knew we were going to mess up, don't you think He already had a plan in place to save us, heal us and restore us?

While you're reading this book, I want you to know and remember, God will take the most traumatic, disgusting, frustrating, conniving, illicit, illegal, detrimental, and life-altering situations and turn them around to serve as our testimonies and deliverance for others.

Romans 8:28 says, "All things work together for good to them who LOVE the Lord and are called according to His purpose." First, we must love Him, and loving Him means we follow His commandments and submit to His will. Then we must understand we are called to His purpose and not our own. Though it's not our place to judge, if we encounter people or know people who are unwilling to admit and accept their brokenness or lack the desire to fix what is wrong or at least be helped, it's possible to believe they are still dealing with some deep-seated issues. What they need is for us to pray for them.

Scabs also keep in those things we need to keep us healthy and to heal. Deep down inside of all of us, there's an innate will to survive. This will is strengthened if we have the proper environment that is conducive and encouraging to us. Emotional scabs help us to keep our hearts tuned to those things that are positive, so we don't lose hope. It helps keep the drive and desire to push forward and progress. It allows us to see if we continue to push forward, continue to do the right thing, if we "Do not become weary of well doing, we will receive our reward from the father who is in heaven." Gal 6:9 (NASB)

Scabs help us see everything we think is finished, isn't over. When our hearts are reeling from the devastation of loss and the pain and anxiety of separation, we can still find the strength to persevere, knowing He has started this great work in our lives and will continue to do so until He returns. Phil 1:6 (NASB) We can find joy in knowing what we're seeing and experiencing is not the end. We can smile because we know a scab is evidence of healing taking place.

Reflections

Psalm 147:3

He heals the brokenhearted and binds up their wounds.

Isaiah 53:5

But he was pierced for our transgressions; he was crushed for our iniquities; upon him was the chastisement that brought us peace and with his wounds we are healed.

2 Chronicles 7:14

If my people who are called by my name humble themselves and pray and seek my face and turn from their wicked ways, then I will hear from heaven and will forgive their sin and heal their land.

Exodus 15:26

If you will diligently listen to the voice of the Lord your God, and do that which is right in his eyes, and give ear to his commandments and keep all his statutes, I will put none of the diseases on you that I put on the Egyptians, for I am the Lord, your healer.

Proverbs 3:8

It will be healing to your body and refreshments to your bones

Psalms 55:22

Cast your burden upon the Lord and He will sustain you; He will never allow the righteous to be shaken

3 John 1:2

Beloved I pray that in all respects you may prosper and be in good health, just as your soul prospers

Write It Down

Learning How To Let Life Hurts Heal

Getting over hurt and disappointment can be hard. What injuries have you sustained in your life? Those caused by others, yourself, or experiences? Be honest with yourself as you reflect. Remember, this is only for you.

Write It Down

Picking Scabs Can Be Painful

Did you allow the "scab" to form or did you remove it prematurely? What happened after that?

Chapter 4

S.P.A.R.

When you hear the word spar, what's the first thing that comes to mind? A boxing match? A wrestling match? I would agree. Being in a match of any kind, normally, two people are within proximity of each other, entangled physically to outdo each other, and gain the victory. Well, my advice to you is when God says no, spar with him, and no, I don't mean to try to physically go to blows with him. I will tell you right now, you will lose! I say that with all honesty and from experience. But spar with him. Accept the challenge to get near him. Get in such proximity, you can feel his breath on your life. Get in so close with Him, you feel his hands on you, turning you, changing you. Get in so close to him, you will be like Jacob as he wrestled with the angel. Tell God, "I am not going to let go until you bless me." As you get close to Him, remember to give Him the respect and honor belonging only to Him because although He is low to the lowly, He is mighty and sovereign. We can never go to God with demands, but we can go to Him with a humble heart full of humility. Let our prayer be, "Any way you bless me, Lord, I'll be satisfied."

How do you spar with God? Surely, we already know we are no match for him, but to come close to him is what he desires. This is what I came up with. Well, I didn't come up with it… this is what God gave me. Don't you love when you're trying to take credit for something and God says, "Nah, not this time."

This acronym is based on the scripture Matthew 7:7, which tells us to, "Ask and it will be given unto you, seek and you shall find, knock and the door will be open."

SEEK

So, the first step in sparring with God is to seek him, not so much to receive an explanation for his answer to our prayers. He owes us no explanation. Second, God is so infinite in all his wisdom, if he did explain it to us, there's no guarantee we would even understand. "His ways are not our ways; his thoughts are not our thoughts." Isaiah 55:8 (NASB) To say we have a total understanding of God is an understatement, but we must seek him to see what his perfect will is for our lives. I'm inclined to believe the cliché that says, "If God says no, it's because he has something better." Now, I know that's no consolation for your displeasure at the beginning, but in due time, if you allow God to work, you will look back and see God was only looking out for you and "Father knows best." Seeking God will take the focus from you and help you to focus on what's important, doing what God desires to bring glory to Him. I hate to burst your bubble, but this life isn't about us. I used to be one of those people who would say, "I'm trying to find myself. I'm searching for my purpose." Our purpose, my purpose, your purpose is for us to worship and glorify God. We were created for His glory, and anything that gets in the way of us acknowledging Him, glorifying Him, and honoring him must go. He will make sure it goes. Exodus 20:5 tells us, God is a jealous God. Not jealous like we get, needing to hold people captive to our desires or needs. God is so jealous of you, He will go where you are to get you, go down as far as you are, and so jealous of you, He gave His only begotten son to die for you. He doesn't want anything or anyone to come before him. He must be number #1!

In times of pain, discomfort, and trouble, one of two things will happen—you will resist God or run to God. And yes, before it's all over, it is possible you will do both. The spirit that dwells within us will only let us resist for so long because the longing to be close to him will take over us. At least, it's my prayer, that's what will happen. So, if you find yourself in a place where you are resisting or have resisted God because of something that happened to you, just know God still loves you. He's waiting for you, and it doesn't matter what it is or how long it's been, he's waiting with his arms open wide. He's waiting for you, wanting you, desiring you, loving you. He's been watching and protecting you, and he can't wait for you to come back to him. He has never left you nor forsaken you. While you have been going through whatever it is you're going through, He's been right there.

Another component of seeking God is it puts us in a position of submission. I know that is a dirty word to some because we don't like to think of ourselves as not being in control, but if you think about it, we're not in control, anyway. The difference is we recognize we don't know it all, don't have all the answers, and He's the only one who does. Even though we are hurt, disappointed, angry, or even puzzled, we submit ourselves to the knowledge of God. We recognize we don't have the power or ability to change our situation without his help. We may start out on a quest to get answers about why things happened the way they did, but there is no way we can get answers from God without getting to know God. I often encourage people to get to *know God* and not just *know about God*. What do I mean? When we *know about God,* we can know Him as the creator of the earth or the one who created us. We know Him in a way told to us or described to us by others. We know Him as the one we pray to or the one we call on in times of trouble. But to *know Him* means we know Him as our Redeemer, the Great I AM. We know Him as the immutable God, one who never changes. We know Him as the one who is Sovereign and righteous beyond all and is the one true and living God. We know Him as Lord and Savior. We know Him intimately. I remember my dad used to have KNOW GOD on his license plate. One day, he was stopped by the police, and when writing out the citation and giving it to my father, my dad noticed the citation read, "NO GOD." How sad there are still people who refuse to acknowledge Jesus Christ is the son of the living God or to even think there are people in this world who have never even heard the good news of Jesus Christ. It's sad when I realize so many people who proclaim to be believers and followers of Christ, only *know about God* but don't really *know God*. When we come to a place of knowing Him, our need to fulfill our self-serving desires will turn into a desire to serve Him.

How do you seek God? If he's already here, and He's not lost, what do you mean by seeking Him? When I say seek Him, look for God in terms of finding Him in His Word. Find out who God is. Find out what He has already promised to do for you. Everything you need is found in the Word of God. There is nothing in this life, in your life, you cannot find an answer to in the Word of God. In order to find the answers, you must read it, study it, take it in, and apply it to your life. You may not know the exact location in the Bible for the answers, but if you dig in and read, one scripture will take you to another scripture, which in turn will apply to other parts of your life, teaching and showing you things you probably didn't imagine you'd learn. If you're just starting your scriptural adventure, I suggest you get a Bible easy to read and understand. Do a little research on which translation works best for you or perhaps ask someone you know who can recommend some options.

During the time God was taking me through my transition period, I dreamed I desired and hungered for God's Word so desperately, I literally began to eat the pages of my Bible. Can you believe that? The dream was so vivid, when I woke up, I had to make sure I hadn't literally eaten my Bible. I literally felt full! I asked God what the dream meant because it seemed so real. He let me know His Word should be taken in, and we should feed on his Word to remain spiritually, mentally, emotionally, and physically fit. I needed that to be able to handle what was coming my way. His Word is the bread of life for us, and He will feed us until we are not hungry anymore, nor will we thirst anymore. We will have no desire for the things of this world but that we will desire Him. Job 23:12 tells us, "I have treasured the words of *His mouth,* more than my necessary food." The Word tells us, "Man will not live by bread alone but by every word that proceeds out of the mouth of God." Matt 4:4 (NASB) Where does the Word of God come from? 2 Timothy 3:16 says, "All scripture is given by inspiration of God and is profitable for doctrine for reproof for correction and instruction in righteousness." So, in other words, God has given us all the clues and directions we need to find Him. To be able to sustain, we must be fully nourished. Just as it's important to be physically fed, we must be spiritually fed.

As a child, when I would get a cold, my mother made sure I would eat. "Feed a cold," she would say. That ensured I had something in my system and on my stomach to maintain my strength. When we are spiritually sick, we must feed our spirit, so we are able to maintain our strength, not that we fight whatever the issue is. "We wrestle not against flesh and blood but against principalities, against powers, against the rulers of the darkness of this age, against spiritual hosts of wickedness in the heavenly places." Eph 6:12 (NASB) There's no way we can fight a spiritual war with natural weapons. "The weapons of our warfare are not carnal…" 2 Cor. 10:4 (NASB) As Pastor Charles Jenkins says in his song, "This means war." Even though the battle has already been won and we are victorious here on earth, until the time we receive our reward in heaven, we must fight and continue to overcome those things that would hinder us from receiving the crown God has reserved with our name on it. Feed your spirit with the Word of God and watch how you will grow.

Reflections

1 Chronicles 16:11

Seek the Lord and his strength; seek his presence continually!

Proverbs 8:17

I love those who love me, and those who seek me diligently find me.

Jeremiah 29:11-14

For I know the plans I have for you, declares the Lord, plans for welfare and not for evil, to give you a future and a hope; Then you will call upon me and come and pray to me, and I will hear you. You will seek me and find me when you seek with all your heart. I will be found by you, declares the Lord, and I will restore your fortunes and gather you from all the nations and all the places where I have driven you, declares the Lord, and I will bring you back to the place from which I sent you into exile.

Luke 11:9-10

And I tell you, ask, and it will be given to you; seek, and you will find; knock, and it will be opened to you. For everyone who asks receives, and the one who seeks finds, and to the one who knocks it will be opened.

Ephesians 6:12

For we wrestle not against flesh and blood, but against principalities, against powers, against the rulers of darkness in this dark age, against the hosts of spiritual wickedness in heavenly places.

Psalms 27:8

When you said, "seek my face," my heart said to You, "Your face, oh Lord. I shall seek."

Psalms 105:3

Glory in His name, let the heart of those who seek the Lord be glad

Write It Down

Look

When we look for something, it's important to have an idea of what we're looking for. What is it that you are looking for God to do?

Pray

As my dad would say, "This is when the rubber meets the road." I can't begin to put in words the importance of prayer. Without prayer, it's pretty much impossible to effectively do any of the other things mentioned in this book—mind you, I used the word effectively. You can go through the motion of doing all the other things, but unless you have developed a line of communication with God, how do you even know if what you're doing is the right thing? How can you do it with the purpose and intent of drawing closer to God if you haven't yet sought His direction? Jesus gave us prayer as the direct way of communicating with him. In the Old Testament, to seek God and get answers from Him, you had to depend on the priests, going into the temple to pray and ask for forgiveness on your behalf. Animals were given as atonement for the wrong you had done. You had to wait on the priests to tell you what it was God was directing you to do. Sometimes, they went into the temple to pray and didn't come out for days. Sometimes, they didn't come out at all. That's why there was a rope tied to them in case they died. The people would pull the rope so that they could pull the body out because they were not allowed into the temple. Can you imagine the level of trust a person must have needed to believe the priest would accurately relay to you what God said? Although they were chosen by God, they were still human and prone to error and sin. So, it was imperative the people of God were obedient and followed Him.

Moses went to the mountain on behalf of the Israelites and didn't come back for forty days. Can you imagine the responsibility of having to go before God with the requests, issues, questions, problems, and dilemmas of everyone, including yourself? Then be responsible for relaying the message from God back to the people, some of which was not pleasing or good news?

There is a story in Mark 9 about the man who brought his son, possessed by a demon, to the disciples for them to pray for him, cast the demon out, and heal him. The disciples were unable to do this, and in frustration, they went to Jesus and asked him why they were unable to cast out the demon in the boy. Jesus told them what they were attempting to do could only come by "fasting and prayer." There are some things we must deal with in life, and the only way we will be able to get through, deal with, overcome, handle, process, or maneuver through it is by prayer.

For those who don't pray a lot, this isn't a reason to stop reading and throw the book away—no cause for alarm. Instead, take a minute and think about the last time you had a deep, intimate conversation with someone you trusted. Think about the time when you laid bare your soul and told them everything you were feeling, and even though they may not have been able to do anything about it, they listened. And after saying all you had to say, you felt better right? Or perhaps you had awesome news you couldn't wait to tell everyone. How did you feel after you shared it, and they rejoiced with you? Didn't it feel good to know others were as happy as you were? Or maybe you had a situation you were unable to talk to anyone about, but you felt if you didn't tell someone, you would literally burst wide open?

Those are just examples but imagine all those scenarios and then some. Instead of them falling to the ground with no results or perhaps dealing with the emotions of all by yourself, imagine there is someone who can do something about every situation, who rejoices every single time you rejoice, who is saddened by every tear you cry, and who can keep each secret. The best thing about it is, you don't have to continue to imagine or daydream whether this person or entity is real. He is very real, and He is waiting for us to bring him every single thing—every situation, problem, hurt, celebration, accomplishment, whatever it is—to Him. How do we take it to Him? In prayer.

Prayer. That word seems to solicit various reactions from people. I often hear people say they don't pray or like to pray because they don't know what to say. Think of how you would talk to a trusted friend or family member and talk to God in the same way, but with a sense of respect and reverence, recognizing even though He is our friend, He is our Heavenly Father. He is holy and sovereign, yet full of love and compassion. Just as we should respect our parents, elders, etc., we should give Him that and even more. I used to talk to my dad about everything. He was my go-to person whenever I needed advice, and whatever advice he gave was usually the best route to take. I didn't always take it, and when I didn't, I wished I had. There wasn't anything I couldn't talk to him about. That's the way it is with prayer. Talking to God is like talking to your best friend. In my case, talking to God is like talking to my dad.

The scripture tells us in Proverbs 18:24, "A man of too many friends comes to ruin, but there is a friend who sticks closer than a brother." 2 Corinthians 6:18 says, "I will be a father to you, and you will be my sons and daughters, says the Lord Almighty." God is that friend. He is that Father. He is that confidant, go-to person who will keep every secret, who always has your back. God is your ride or die. Because of the crucifixion and the resurrection, we are now able to go to God on our own.

Prayer is the form of communication God has given us to deal directly with him. We can go directly to Him, sit before Him, and pour out our heart to Him. We no longer have to share our deepest darkest secrets with someone else for them to take them to God. We no longer must hide our guilt and shame, and we don't have to worry if what we're talking to God about is trivial. He cares about everything that concerns us. He tells us 1 Peter 5:7 to "Cast our cares upon Him because He cares for us." So, by praying, we can give Him everything in our lives that concerns us and have confidence, knowing He can do something about each and everything we bring to Him.

In parent/children relationships, there is an unequal exchange of "benefits." Children are more than likely to receive abundantly more from their parents than what they give their parents. They attempt to show their appreciation through hugs, kisses, gifts, and other expressions of forgiveness. They haven't grown to the point, they understand love is shown not only in material things but through the love, respect, and reverence they give to their parents. As a child of God, and even for the unbeliever, we receive abundantly more than what we give back to God. That is the beauty of being in a relationship with Him. Even in our meager attempts to please Him with our gifts, tithes, and offerings, it is a relationship He desires—a heart willing to serve Him and a spirit that desires to give Him free rein in our, so He may receive the glory.

So, I know it seems like I got off focus, but I said all of that to say this. Prayer is your way of going to God and asking him for guidance and clarification about what He has said. Look at it like this. If you were sitting in class and the teacher said something you didn't understand, would you just sit there and not ask questions, leaving yourself to remain confused and unable to pass the test at the required time? Or would you ask for clarification and understanding? When I was growing up, my parents would answer my questions about their authority with "Because I said so," and that was the end of that conversation. I recognize we live in different times, and children are always asking why, and instead of being satisfied with "Because I said so," they want clarification. The same way we seek clarification in other areas of our lives, God desires we seek Him for clarification. He desires we ask Him questions, and in times of disappointment, hurt, and inability to understand, He wants us to come to Him and to be comfortable, not only asking why but also asking what do we need to do differently? We also must be content and satisfied in Him when He responds, "Because I said so." Prayer is not just a way for us to question God about His decisions or will in our lives but an opportunity to see where we need to make changes. Prayer is the way we can have an intimate private conversation with God about anything and everything. There is nothing off-limits we can't talk to Him about. Inasmuch as I enjoyed every conversation with my father, he wasn't always able to solve my problems or answer my questions. When I go to God in prayer, I know the answer He gives—because He always has an answer—will be in the best interest for my life.

Using prayer when we have received an unfavorable answer from God also allows us to draw closer to him, so we can once again see his good and perfect will for our lives. Maybe what you desire from God is in his will, just not at that time. For example, you're praying for a new job and go on a job interview. You felt like the interview was awesome and are excited. You think there's no way you won't get the position, the employer all but said that the job was yours. But then you get the call or the letter that you weren't selected. What do you do? You met the qualifications. You dressed the part. You said the right thing. You prayed, and they still turned you down. Why God? God knows you need the job, and it was perfect, or so you thought, yet he still didn't allow you to get it. That is when we must dig in and trust God enough to know though He desires to give us what we desire, he is only going to give us what is best for us when it's best for us.

Acts 13:22 refers to David as "A man after God's own heart." David understood the importance of seeking God and knowing what God desired from him even after he had fallen. Prayer helps us understand God's heart. When we pray and meditate on Gods'

Word, we can do things that for others are impossible. Like the disciples who were unable to cast out the demon, without prayer, there are some things we wouldn't be able to handle or understand. If we can't fully understand, through prayer, we will learn to trust whatever God is doing at that time of our life is okay.

Think of this. Being fully God and fully man, Jesus Christ was prayed to as Lord, but as a man, He prayed. There are different times in the Bible, where it mentions Jesus praying. Even in His praying to God the Father, He learned to be obedient unto the will of His father, even unto death. If Jesus had to pray, what makes us think we can survive this life, filled with transitions, without praying. If Jesus, who was God and the son of God, humbled Himself enough to pray, sought His heavenly Father, and was obedient, what makes us think we should not humble ourselves and seek God and be obedient? If anything, we should be so even more!

By now, you may be asking, "What if I don't know how to pray?" God knew we would come into difficulty in our prayer lives, so He gave us the Model Prayer when He gave it to the disciples. The disciples, people who were spending time daily in the physical presence of Jesus, even asked, "Father teach us to pray…" Luke 11:1 (NIV) The prayer Jesus gave us to pray covers all the things we need to pray about, even if it seems to be vague.

"Our Father" is recognition as to who God is in our lives. If He is our father, then He is the head of our lives and the one we can turn to as a parent in our lives.

"Which art in heaven" lets us know our Father is in heaven. God created the heavens and the earth, and heaven is where He is waiting for us on the day we shall join him there.

"Hallowed be thy name" is reverencing God. Blessed is the name of Jesus! His name is holy, wonderful, and majestic.

"Thy kingdom come, thy will be done on earth as it is in heaven" is asking that God's will be done in our lives as we experience His kingdom here on earth as His kingdom is in heaven. We are to establish kingdom lifestyles. Let the power of God reign and have dominion, just as it does in the heavens.

"Give us this day our daily bread" is asking for what we need for this day. We are not to worry about what we need for tomorrow or the next day. When the Israelites were in the wilderness, God fed them with manna from heaven. He instructed them to only gather what they needed for the day. He doesn't want us to be worried or concerned about what we will eat, drink, or wear. He wants us to trust Him for what we need daily, and that applies to everything in our lives.

"Forgive us our debts as we forgive our debtors" lets us know we are to not only ask for forgiveness for ourselves, but we would also forgive those who have done things to us. Col 3:13 lets us know, "We must forgive as God has also forgiven us."

"Lead us not into temptation." God does not tempt us, so there is no way He will lead us into doing anything that goes against His word.

James 1:13 tells us, "Let no man say when he is tempted, I am tempted of God, for God cannot be tempted with evil, neither tempteth he any man."

"But deliver us from all evil," is asking God to save us from everything that will harm us, cause us harm, cause us to stray, etc. In His delivering us from evil, He lets us know we will be tempted, but 1 Corinthians 10:13 tells us, "No temptation has overtaken you but such as is common to man; and God is faithful, who will not allow you to be tempted beyond what you are able, but with the temptation will provide the way of escape that you will be able to endure it."

"For Thine is the kingdom and the power and the glory." God has established His kingdom and reigns with all power and glory. Therefore, we know there is nothing that happens or goes on in this life, God is not in control of.

So, in this prayer, we can address our praise to God, our needs to God, and our need for help from God. There are many people who say you can use an acronym to help when in prayer: A.C.T.S.

A-adoration to God. "Our Father, who are in heaven hallowed be Thy name, Thy kingdom come, Thy will be done."

C-confess your sins. "Lead us not into temptation but deliver us from evil."

T-Thank God for all His blessings to you because all we are and have is because of Him and His divine power. "For Thine is the kingdom, the power, and the glory."

S- Supplication, asking God for what we need, "Give us this day our daily bread." That is not the only way to pray. We have already established prayer is a conversation between you and God. But if you are having a bit of trouble getting started, hopefully, this will help.

Prayer is not only a way of getting closer to God in times of confusion or trouble but also a wonderful way of just talking to God as a friend, a confidante, and a release. Sometimes, you just want to talk to God about stuff you may have found puzzling or even funny, or you may want clarification about something you read and need a little more understanding. God isn't only available when life is turning upside down. He is there in good times and wants to hear all about them. He wants to laugh with you and rejoice with you. He wants you to tell Him about what you experienced at work that brought a smile to your face or to hear you say "Thank you, Lord" when you got that good parking space at the store or when you looked at your family, and they were all healthy and safe. That's a prayer. Whether verbal or just a thought, that's a prayer, and that's talking to God. That's all He wants.

Reflections

1 John 5:14-15

And this is the confidence that we have toward him, that if we ask anything according to his will, he will hear us. And if we know that he hears us in whatever we ask, we know that we have the requests that we have asked of him.

Thessalonians 5:16-18

Rejoice always, pray without ceasing, give thanks in all circumstances, for this is the will of God in Christ Jesus for you.

Jeremiah 33:3

Call to me and I will answer you, and will tell you great and hidden things that you have not known.

Write It Down

What do you think?

What does s mean to you?

Write It Down

Let's Make it Happen

What are ways you can incorporate more prayer into your life?

Write It Down

What's the Point?

When it seems as though our prayers are not being answered, we begin to wonder if it is even worth it. Do you feel prayer is necessary? Why or why not?

My Prayers	God's Answers

Ask

Ask, ask, ask. Did your parents ever tell you, all you did was ask for stuff? Or have you ever said that to someone else? Do you have people in your life that it seems **EVERY** time you turn around, they're asking for something? Does that frustrate you? I imagine it does. I have dealt with people who the time I only saw or heard from them was when they were asking me for something. I would get frustrated and inwardly groan when I saw them coming. Asking goes hand in hand with prayer. As you are praying, you're making your requests known unto God. Aren't you glad God doesn't groan when He sees you coming? I'm glad because I know I can get worrisome, but God wants us to keep coming. He wants us to ask, over and over and over and over and over… I think you've got it. He said in Matthew 7:7, "Ask, and it shall be given unto you." Now, before you get excited or upset, this doesn't mean just because you ask for something, you're going to get it. As I said before, God isn't a vending machine god, nor is He a genie in the bottle. If we go over to 1 John 5:14, it says, "And this is the confidence we have that if we ask anything *According to His Will,* He will hear us and because He hears us, He will give us what it is we petition for." Do you see what the keywords are? *According to His Will.* So, there we have it. We can ask for whatever we want, anything, and He will hear us. Not only will He hear us, He will give us what we are asking for as long as we are asking for it according to His will. Note, it doesn't say our will or our wants, but His will.

A part of being able to cross the bridge from our pain to purpose is coming to the point of understanding we need God, and we need to ask Him what we want. We can't get around it. We can act like we don't. We can walk around as though we have everything under control, but truth be told, even to do those things we shouldn't, God allows it. For us to do and receive what we need, we must ask Him for His help. The songwriter says, "Without God, I can do nothing. Without Him, I would fail. Without God, my life would be rugged, like a ship without a sail."

I've told you to bring your desires, needs, wants, and issues to God, and He will give you what you pray for, but then I say, He won't always give us what we ask for. Then comes the big question—why keep asking? If we are sincere in our seeking and our praying, our asking will eventually line up with what God desires for us. In other words, when His will becomes our will, we will desire what He has for us, and nothing else will be acceptable. Okay, so maybe you aren't satisfied with that explanation about asking. Let's look at James 4:2-3, "You have not because you ask not. But then when you do ask, you don't receive because you're asking with the wrong motives..." So, we should always ask God for whatever we want with the belief He will give us what we are asking for with the intent of glorifying Him and receiving His will. Are we really asking for what we want, or are we asking Him to tell us what we need to want, so we will be in line with what He wanted us to have in the first place?

If God knows what we need or want before we ask for it, what is the purpose of asking? Asking draws us into a closer relationship with God. Asking in prayer will allow us to abide in God, and He abides in us, and when that happens, we will be able to ask whatever we wish, and it will be done for us. John 15:7 (NIV)

Why do we ask? The Bible tells us to, Jesus tells us to. Remember when I mentioned how frustrating it is when someone keeps asking you something over and over? Or when we asked our parents over and over for something, then were disappointed when we didn't get it? Asking is recognizing and reverencing God as sovereign and supplier. Asking is recognizing our need for Him daily. Asking is humbling ourselves to an all-powerful God who cares about us more than the birds of the air. God never gets tired of us coming to Him and asking Him for anything. He never gets tired of us calling on His name. He never gets frustrated when we pray the same prayer, even if He has answered the prayer, and we haven't received the answer. He still wants us to ASK HIM!!! He wants us to come to Him because He knows He can do something about the situation you're dealing with. We ask Him because trying to do things on our own can cause us stress and anxiety.

He tells us in Philippians 3:5-7, "Be anxious for nothing (don't stress about anything), but in everything by prayer and supplication (by asking in prayer) with thanksgiving (be thankful) make your requests known unto God (tell Him what you need/desire) and the peace that passes all understanding (a calmness you can't explain) will guard your heart and mind through Christ Jesus (will help you remain calm and trust that God will take care of everything.)" He can cause you to get the job you desire. He can rescue you from the trouble you're facing. He can heal you of the sickness you're battling. He doesn't want you to go elsewhere, trying to fix it on your own, nor does He want you trying to get others to solve problems they are unable to handle.

My mother once told me when I was a child, "Don't ask your friends to solve your problems. They're kids too, and they haven't lived any longer than you have. They don't know any more than you do." So, why would we take our problems to others who can't handle their own problems? Yes, our family, friends, coworkers, other people are good to listen and offer support or advice, but to deal with the root of the problem, God is the only one who can bring about foolproof and legitimate change. He's the only one who can heal you. He's the only one who can keep you from going insane. He's the one who provides the resources for you to be able to get the food you need. He's the one who can mend your broken heart after a bad relationship. He knows He is the only one who can fix your problem and wants you to bring Him your problem and ask Him to fix it for you.

Reflections

Matthew 21:22

And whatever you ask in prayer, you will receive, if you have faith.

1 Chronicles 16:11

Seek the Lord and his strength; seek his presence continually.

Psalms 107:6

Then they cried to the Lord in their trouble, and he delivered them from their distress.

Psalm 5:12

Give ear to my words, O Lord; consider my groaning. Give attention to the sound of my cry, my King and my God, for to you do I pray.

Write It Down

Dealing with it

How do you handle asking for tangible things from a God who you cannot physically see?

Write It Down

What Is It You Really Want

What are your motives for the things you pray for?

Receive

You would think this should be the easy part of the process. It's easy to receive good news, right? We all like to receive blessings, favor, promotions, etc., but no one likes to receive unpleasant things. We don't like answers or results, not in our favor. We don't like being told we can't have or can't do something. Being told no makes us feel we are being denied. I'll say again, as a believer, I almost felt entitled. I thought with everything I had been through, I was entitled to a yes. Because I had changed my ways, God would be proud and say oh, she's doing so good now, I'll give her what she wants. I was treating folks right. I was bridling my tongue. I wasn't going off the handle like I used to. I was learning how to forgive. I was on a roll. The problem with all of this is, I wasn't putting faith in God that he would do what was best for me. I was putting faith in what I thought I needed to do for God to give me what I wanted. Kinda sounds like I was trying spiritual manipulation, right? When I realized God answering my prayer was not predicated on my works, I was able to receive what He was showing me. Then I was able to begin to maturely process my situation. One scripture that comes to mind is when Job had become ill, and his wife was ridiculing him. He says to her, "Should we accept good from God and not trouble?" Job 2:10 (NIV)

Life is full of swift transitions, full of trouble and trials, but it's also full of blessings, joy, and happiness. How do you prepare yourself to handle the good with the bad? Or should I say, how do you prepare yourself to receive the bad? How do you "take a lickin' and keep on tickin'?" What puts us in the right position to receive? When your heart and mind are on the same page, it makes it easier for your emotions/feelings/spirit to receive what God is saying. For example, if I am hurting or disappointed because of being denied something for a reason, it may be a bit difficult to receive what I perceive as the next best thing. In the eyes of God, everything He gives us is top-notch! It is #1.

What if your emotions/feelings/spirit aren't on the same page just yet? That's when the seeking, praying, and asking part comes into play. To receive all He has to give us, we must seek Him and find out what He wants from us. What an interesting concept. For us to be able to receive, we must first find out what we need to give. Being able to give of ourselves, so we can receive puts us in a position of submission. We must trust God enough to give him everything we have and are faced with, so in turn, He can give us what we need. In waiting for him to give us what we need, we continuously seek him to find out what more he wants. As we submit to him and what he wants, we become more excited about what he is going to do in our lives. To believe what we will receive from him is in our best interest, our hearts and minds must be on the same page. In our healing process, just as we get new skin over our injuries, we become new creatures. Therefore, we have a different way of feeling, thinking, and seeing things. Once we are renewed and born again in Christ Jesus, old things, old thinking, old feelings, old actions are no longer a part of who we are. All things become new. When all things become new, we are open in our spirit to receive all God has for us.

Being able to receive means, we have a heart of gratitude. When we know each and everything we receive from God will be nothing short of his best, we can receive whatever He gives with thanksgiving. Even if whatever he gives us or allows is painful, we can find joy and a reason to be thankful. Again remember, everything that's good *for* us doesn't feel good *to* us.

Once you have received God's gift of grace and mercy, you will no longer be content with just anything. In other words, we won't be so quick to run back to those things that caused us the problems. It's like being upgraded—once we get used to having the best, we won't settle for anything less.

After you have begun to have a real and sincere relationship with God, once you have begun to know your worth, once you have begun to understand you can have and do far greater than what your mind can imagine, you won't settle for just any old thing. You won't believe you can just do okay. You won't just think mediocre thoughts. You begin to think out-of-this-world thoughts. You begin to not only believe you are victorious, you begin to live victoriously. You begin to believe God is able to do exceedingly and abundantly above all you can ask or think.

So often I hear people say, Lord, give me peace or give me joy. The scripture tells us Jesus has already given us peace. He has already given us his peace, and it's up to us to receive it and to walk in it. I believe we are able to ask how we can receive it. I believe we must learn how to live in peace and how to walk in the knowledge that God is our peace. Therefore, if we accept God, we have accepted His peace. We have access to receive what God has for us, we just must put ourselves in a position to receive.

To receive, we must also empty ourselves. Have you ever been pouring something and not been paying attention? The liquid begins to overflow because you continued to pour into a container that was already full. There is no way we can expect to be filled with the things of God if we are already so full of everything else. If we are continuously filling our hearts and minds with natural things, there is no room for anything spiritual. If we are full of unresolved issues, emotions, feeling, thoughts, desires, wants, needs, likes, dislikes, issues, regrets, failures, judgments, and so much other stuff, there is no room for us to be able to allow Jesus to dwell within us. We can't receive Him if there's too much of us in the way. Make some room for Him. All He needs is for you to say, "Yes, you can come in," and that's it. You must RECEIVE Him into your heart and life to be able to handle everything else life tries to throw at you.

While you are in a position of waiting with God and for God, that is a season you can give unto others. My mother used to tell me, "As long as you keep your hands so tightly closed, you won't let anything out, but you also don't let anything in." Being anxious and upset about the things you feel you didn't get from God will cause you to miss out on the opportunity to be thankful for the things YOU HAVE ALREADY RECEIVED from God.

How often have you heard, it's better to give than to receive? They say it often in church during the offering. Guess what? It's true, and not only when giving money. To give to others does something to change your outlook and situation. When you give freely and willingly, not grudgingly, you put yourself in a place of submission. There's that word again—submission. You are submitting yourself to God to allow Him to mold you. You can learn and observe the characteristics of God. As we learn more about the characteristics of God and who He is and how we should be emulating Him, we become full of those things of Him. As David stated in Psalm 23, "My cup runneth over." When our cups run over with the goodness of God, it will pour out into the lives of others and our situation. That's your way of giving. Let me tell you, there is no way the spirit of God will overflow into your situation and not cause something to change! All the while, you're asking God to meet you in your situation, you are adding to the lives of others. You are bringing about change to others. You may not navigate your situation the way you think you should, but while you are going through and continuing to share with others, it will help you find peace as you wait.

Reflections

Mark 11:24

Therefore, I tell you, whatever you ask in prayer, believe that you have received it, and it will be yours.

Philippians 4:19

And my God will supply every need of yours according to his riches in glory in Christ Jesus.

James 1:17

Every good gift and every perfect gift is from above, coming down from the Father of lights, with whom there is no variation or shadow due to change.

John 15:7

If you abide in me, and my words abide in you, ask whatever you wish, and it will be done for you.

Write It Down

Take a Look in the Mirror

We all have something we are full of. Reflect on those things that seem to be taking up space in your lives. What are you willing to give up to receive what God has for you?

Chapter 5

EAT YOUR VEGETABLES

My parents made me eat my vegetables, not because they necessarily tasted good or because I enjoyed them. Truth be told, there were very few vegetables I enjoyed then nor enjoy now. As a matter of fact, stewed tomatoes and okra was a dish I vowed if I ever got grown, I was never eating, and to this day, I don't eat okra, unless they're fried. Growing up, I didn't have a choice; my parents were totally not interested in what I liked or didn't like. They were not moved by the fact I had an opinion about what I thought was best for me. Because they knew what was best for me and I wasn't old enough or experienced enough to understand the importance of eating properly and healthy, it was their responsibility to instruct me what was best.

That's what God does. That's what His Word does. He knows we can't determine what's best for ourselves, so He guides us and directs us what we should do and what will bring us the best benefit. If He had created us with all the answers, we would not need Him, and He would not have given us the Bible, His written Word of instructions to navigate this life. If we didn't need guidance, He would not have sent his Holy Spirit to comfort us and "teach us in all things." It's in the times of decision-making, we should defer to Him and what He wants to do in our lives.

When we have questions or need answers, we use Google, Alexis, Siri, or maybe family and friends, but when it comes down to getting information about ourselves, who do we turn to? When we need to find out about us, where do we go? Perhaps we should do a spiritual Google with God and inquire. What does He want *from* us? What does He want *for* us? Like our parents and those who love us, He wants us to take in good things, so we will grow and mature, not to stay as babes. When we first came into our relationship with Christ, we were as babes. We knew much of nothing about Him in relation to who He was and what He wanted from us, what He was going to do or able to do in our lives, and how to come to Him for what we needed. As we studied His Word and sat in His presence, we began to grow, and in our growing, we began to get a better idea of what God desires for us to do to better serve His purpose and glorify Him. Some of you reading this book may find yourself still as a babe in Christ, and that's okay. Reading this book, lets me know you want to grow. You desire to mature in Christ, and that's exactly what He wants.

When we were growing up, we all started out in kindergarten or preschool. As we grew and learned, we were promoted. As we were promoted, we learned what we should and should not do. We learned what was best for us and began to realize it was best we didn't behave a certain way because we were getting older. Certainly, in the third grade, we didn't whine or cry when our parents left us as we might have in kindergarten. We learned it was best for us to stay in school and learn. We didn't necessarily like it, but we didn't have a choice, it was for our good. If we asked if we could stay home, we were told no, not because our parents didn't love us or enjoy our company, but going to school was what we needed. We were not old enough or experienced enough to understand—and the law required otherwise. We couldn't make that decision on our own as what we felt was best. Until you reach a certain age, you can't logically and rationally make the decision whether you need an education. When it comes to our relationship with God, He knows there are some things we are just not mature enough to handle. There are some decisions we cannot make on our own. I see plenty of things on social media that make me wonder if people take any thought before posting things… but that's another subject.

As children of God, He knows we are constantly growing, learning, and will make mistakes along the way. He knows we need his infinite wisdom and guidance daily. He also knows, no matter how he desires to lead us in the right direction, there are going to be times when we are not going to want what's best for us. We are not going to want "to eat our vegetables." We aren't going to care about growth or improvement. We will get to a point where we want to stop doing the right thing, but even when not if, but when we do, He is there, always forgiving, always loving, always patient, and still telling us to "eat our vegetables."

When I was made to eat the okra and tomatoes, they tasted disgusting. I didn't like the texture, and just looking at them would make me gag. When I asked why I had to eat them, not only was I told, "Because I said so," I was told, even though I thought they didn't taste or look good, they were good for me. Isn't that how God operates in our lives? We are forced to go through some disgusting situations, situations that don't feel good, are not enjoyable, and are downright full of anguish. I hear God saying, even though it may not be pleasing to us, it will work for our good. Romans 8:28 tells us, "All things work together for good to them that love the Lord and are called according to His purpose." So, that job loss, divorce, death, or unexpected illness will work for your good. How is that, you ask?

Our purpose is to worship God, not to worry. By worshiping God, it takes the focus from us and puts it on Him. By putting the focus on Him, we are so consumed with Him, it then allows Him to do what He needs to do in our lives. As we are in worship and He is at work, we will be able to see how He can turn things around for us. What we thought were denial and defeat, turn into a dynamic destiny. We can then sing as the songwriter, "Whatever my lot, thou has taught me to say, it is well… it is well… with my soul."

Reflections

Proverbs 8:35

For whoever finds me finds life and obtains favor from the LORD,

Isaiah 40:28

Have you not known? Have you not heard? The LORD is the everlasting God, the Creator of the ends of the earth. He does not faint or grow weary; his understanding is unsearchable.

Proverbs 9:10

The fear of the LORD is the beginning of wisdom, and the knowledge of the Holy One is insight.

Proverbs 2:6

For the LORD gives wisdom; from his mouth come knowledge and understanding.

Write It Down

Can't see the sun for the clouds

It's hard to see the silver lining in disappointing situations. How can you turn what seems to be a negative situation into something positive?

Write It Down

What Do You SEE?

Can you see anything good in your situation? How can you use that to grow stronger?

Chapter 6

CHANGE YOUR MIND

I'm stubborn. I'm strong-willed. I'm persistent and point-blank stubborn. I like what I like, and yes, I will admit it, I want what I want when I want it. To some, that classifies as not being just stubborn but spoiled. Okay, so maybe I'm stubborn and spoiled, but what I am learning to do is change my mind. Does changing my mind make me less spoiled or stubborn? Nope, it sure doesn't, but what I have learned is to think about things differently and change my approach. I must stop and think, is what I want that important? How will it add or take away from my life? Is it really that serious? Now, I don't always think that immediately, I'm not always in a rational mode, but when I am, I'm better able to think things through—this comes from eating my vegetables. Sometimes, others must help me to be rational.

Okay, a moment of transparency—I deal with bouts of depression Before you get all worked up and say how saved people don't ge depressed, etc., let me first say, depression is real. Many of you reading this book may suffer from depression, and some of you may be depressed and not even know it. But that's for my next book (lol) But back to me. So, yes, I deal with depression, and before God started giving me this book to write, I was going through a major battle—crying from early morning unto the evening, not eating, losing weight, headaches—the whole kit and caboodle, as my mother would say. What's even worse is I got to the point, no one knew how depressed I was, how I was dying inside, how bad the fight was that was inside of me. I was fighting the depression, but I was also fighting God. I was having a temper tantrum in my spirit and was not willing to let go of what I wanted, even though I knew I would receive better than what I thought I wanted. With His wisdom and guidance, I was better able to get the help I needed through a professional counselor. Yes, God uses various things: people, medicines, therapists, counselors, to help us to heal.

As much as I was praying, He wasn't even trying to take the desire from me. He could have very easily changed my heart, my desire, my mind, and forced His will upon me, but being the gentleman He is, He allowed me to cry, fight, squirm, moan, groan, complain, and run headfirst into the brick wall! Now, what kind of kind, loving, gentle God, who cares about me, would do that? The kind who knows until I changed my mindset toward Him, He would not be able to change me. The kind who knew until I was ready to do what He wanted me to do, I was of no use to anyone else. The kind who knew once I came to my senses, there would be no stopping, no regretting, and no turning back.

Have you ever been hurt or angry, and the person you're upset with tries to hug you? You get into this bit of a tussle because they're trying to hold you, and you're in a place of resistance and submission. You want them to hold you, but you're so upset, you don't want them to touch you, but in the end, you give in and let them hold you, and it feels good. It was, in all actuality, what you wanted and needed.

So, how did I get to the point where I was able to get it together? Or at least to the point that I could survive without being driven by anger, vengeance, hate, and hurt? I had to change my mind. Did I change my mind about what I wanted? In a way, but not entirely. Well, at least not from the beginning. I began to change my mind about how I was going to deal with what I was feeling. I began to gradually see for me to come out on the other side, for me to cross the bridge to where I needed to be in Christ, for me to navigate all that was going on and function, I would have to intentionally allow God to BE God. I had to be honest and truthful with myself about what I was feeling. There was no need to lie to myself and God when He already knew. How can you be treated for an illness if you refuse to tell the physician what's wrong? I had to change my mind, and I'm still learning how to go about doing things.

My mother used to tell me when I was dealing with certain things, "When you get tired of being sick and tired, you'll do something different." Well, I got to the point, I was sick and tired of being sick and tired. I was tired of crying, tired of pleading, tired of begging. I was sick and tired of praying, and nothing seemed to be changing—but prayers *were* being answered. The Bible tells us we don't know what to pray for, so the Holy Spirit intercedes on our behalf, Thank God for that. I was tired of what I was putting myself through and made up in my mind I needed peace. Not that I didn't still want what my flesh wanted, but how do you get peace when what your flesh wants is contrary to what God wants? You can't. God must have the final say. My goal was to receive peace because my mind couldn't take it anymore. Peace was no longer an option. It became a must, a life-and-death issue, my air to breathe, my need to function. I had to have peace. I began to pray over my mind.

Isaiah 26:3 tells us, "You keep him (her) in perfect peace whose mind is stayed on you because he trusts in You." I began to ask God to help me trust Him. I began to ask Him to change me. Don't change the people. Don't change the situation or the circumstance. If God were to change the situation or the circumstance to suit me, but I never changed my actions or my thoughts, when the next unpleasant situation comes about, I would not be able to handle it and would need Him to change it. I needed Him to change me. If He changed me, I knew I could handle whatever happened after that. I had to begin to trust that His love for me outweighed whatever it was I thought I wanted to do. I had to shift my thinking from what does laine want to what does God want? I realized, usually, if we want omething so badly and it's difficult coming to fruition and causing ure-T H-E double hockey sticks, maybe we should go back to God nd see if what we're doing is truly His will.

'hat doesn't always mean we're out of His will completely, but it ever hurts to get confirmation about what He wants us to do. I am earning I must love God more than I love me and to love me more han I love what my body and mind may want. Philippians 2:5-6 tells ıs, "Let this same attitude and purpose and (humble) mind be in ou which was in Christ Jesus (let Him be your example in humility) And do not be conformed to this world, but be transformed by the enewing of your mind, so that you may prove what the will of God s, that which is good and acceptable and perfect." When we begin o see things how God would want us to see them, when we begin o think the way Christ thinks, we are in a better position to be what He wants and to do those things that will show the world what God wants and those that things are "good, acceptable, and perfect."

Changing your mind about how you see things helps you to change how you deal with things. The changing of your mind does not negate what you think you want; it helps you look at the situation more clearly. We must remember, God is not a god of confusion, nor will He tempt us. We are tempted when we are enticed and lured by our own desires. 1 Cor 14:33 tells us, "God is not a God of disorder but of peace, as in all the congregations of the of the Lord's people." 1 Corinthians 14:33 (NIV) Confusion happens when what is true and what we think to be true are in conflict. Sometimes, the problem comes in when we can't readily figure out which is which. The enemy loves to bring us enticing options to confuse us and keep us from being able to think clearly. God is not going to confuse or tempt us. He is going to be clear, even if, in His clarity, we are not able to initially understand. He knows we are not capable of fully understanding what He is doing initially. He is gracious enough, He will send us the information in bits and pieces, so it eventually, it all falls into place. I found if I allowed myself to be enticed and led by what my heart and mind wanted, I stayed in a state of confusion, trying to figure things out. I will admit, there were times I wanted to give up and throw in the towel. I was tired of trying to figure things out. I was tired of making a step in what I thought was the right direction, only to find out it was the wrong direction. I decided since everything else I had tried wasn't working, why not allow God to have His way?

I encourage you as you continue this journey, crossing bridge to bridge, to allow God to lead you and have His way. If you, too, have been trying all sorts of things to try to get your life to come together, let Him have a stab at things. It certainly won't hurt. You will have difficulties, trials, hurts, and pain, but it's so much easier when you know, no matter what you're facing, He's going to be right there, not just as a spectator but as an active advocate for you. You will have your very own #1 fan, rooting for you the entire time. Malachi 3:10 says, "Test me and see if I will not open the windows of heaven for you and pour down for you blessings until there is no more need." Even though this is used mostly about finances, I can't help but believe and apply it to every aspect of my life. God is saying to us, "Trust me, try me. I got you. I won't let you down. I won't let you fall. Watch what I will do." He can do exceedingly and abundantly above what we can ask or think, but first, we must decide to make a conscious effort to change our minds.

Write It Down

Change your mind

Take a minute and think of some things you are just set in your ways about. It could be relationships, the way we speak or think. Is there a habit you just can't or don't want to break, but if you did, it would help? It could be something as simple as changing your eating habits or exercising. Ask God to reveal to you how you're thinking about them and write them down. Then ask God to help you change your mind and the way you think, so you will "have the mind of Christ Jesus."

Chapter 7

FORGIVE

This chapter was THE absolute hardest to write. I juggled my thoughts around so much with this because I couldn't figure out how forgiveness had anything to do with dealing with God's response of "no" in our lives. So, I'm going to try to relay it to you the way God gave it to me. When I was younger, my parents would drive down to Washington, D.C., to visit my maternal grandfather. Every time we left to head back home, my grandfather would give my brother and me money to stop at a corner store to buy ice cream. That was one of the highlights of the trip, and I looked forward to that treat.

Well, one time, we went in, and my brother was digging through the containers of ice cream, looking for the one he wanted. Mind you, we were kids, so in his mind, all he wanted was the ice cream. We had never had any problems with the store owner, never exchanged any harsh or disrespectful words. My parents let us go in by ourselves. But this day, he said something to my brother about digging through all the containers of ice cream. Perhaps he had just straightened them. Perhaps he didn't want them left disheveled or that day just wasn't his day. Perhaps he wasn't feeling well. Whatever the reason, on that day, he didn't want my brother to dig through his containers of ice cream, and he made it known. Instead of my brother making attempts to straighten them or say anything rude, he left, just walked out of the store. Neither he nor I got any ice cream that day. As a matter of fact, we never stopped there again. My brother said he never wanted ice cream from there again, so my parents never stopped again. Now, I had no problem going back there, but my parents honored his wishes and allowed those feelings of anger to grow and fester. When I reflect on what happened, I wonder why my parents didn't go in and address the situation. Had it even been that serious? My brother didn't seem to realize his anger toward the store clerk over the ice cream not only affected himself, but the store clerk and me as well. I was not able to enjoy something my grandfather had wanted me to have, and the store clerk lost two loyal customers. Would my parent's intervention have helped? I know it certainly would have helped me. Now that I'm writing this, it makes me wonder, do I have some unresolved issues regarding it? I mean, I was affected by my brother not wanting to go back and by my parents not addressing it, so I would still be able to go and enjoy my ice cream. Was this stand of solidarity helpful? Often, we have feelings about something we didn't even know were still there. We may say we're good, and we don't feel anything, but if you can't go in the store because the clerk who looked at you wrong is working there, you have something you need to deal with. Or perhaps that person that cheated on you or someone at church said something to your child you don't appreciate. Did you realize church hurt is one of the main reasons so many people don't go to church? There are plenty of other scenarios I could use, but I think you get the point. Unforgiveness is a slow-eating spiritual cancer that manifests itself in physical experiences.

For years, my brother talked ill about the store clerk, making me realize he didn't want to apologize to me if no one else. At that time, I felt like he owed me an apology. I still wanted ice cream. I didn't have a problem, he did. He didn't want to forgive, even if it didn't seem like he hadn't done wrong. That's when I realized I needed to forgive because I felt like he owed me something. I hadn't let go and felt I was owed an apology. See how unforgiveness just sneaks in?

If you feel someone owes you an apology, you have unforgiveness to deal with. If you continuously get upset over something they did, it's possible you have unforgiveness to deal with. Holding other people hostage in your heart does nothing to them. He felt wronged, the store clerk felt wronged, I felt wronged. As long as we hide behind self-frustration about who did us wrong, we will never be able to move on and receive those other blessings in life.

We continued to visit my grandfather but never went back to the store. The story about the store has become something my family and I laugh at sometimes. Don't we sometimes laugh to hide what's really bothering us or just because we don't feel like it's a big deal? In that situation, no, it's not a big deal to me; well, at least not anymore. What about those situations that are big deals, we don't or won't address? They must be addressed so you can be free. My father used to tell me just because you don't deal with an issue doesn't mean it's gone away. The weight you've been feeling maybe something someone has done to you that they haven't apologized for. You may never get an apology, but you still are required to forgive. Sometimes, people have hurt or offended us, and they don't even realize they've done so.

The store clerk may not have even missed our stops or our presence. Our monthly dollars may not even have made a difference in the store's profits, but the situation still lingers with me. I don't know if it lingers with my brother after all these years. When I go to visit my aunt and uncles now, I drive past that old store. The store is closed, but in my mind, I go back to that little girl, eagerly waiting to receive my dollar so I can go to the store for my ice cream. I don't feel anger or animosity. I just remember that's the store where my brother got upset because the clerk didn't want him to move his ice cream around. I'm chuckling now… wow.

Unforgiveness becomes a cage, which we lock ourselves in, tightly holding onto the key, yet blaming others for being locked up. When we are dealing with denials in our lives, we must decide to forgive.

Forgiveness is just another step you take in crossing the bridge. When I started writing this chapter, I really thought God was going to shed some light on the situation I had been dealing with regarding my divorce and my need to forgive. A pain I had never felt, it left me bitter, angry, frustrated, and feeling rejected and abandoned. I thought I was feeling all of that because of what had happened to me from the divorce and other failed relationships, but by writing about forgiveness, God showed me I was harboring unforgiveness from what I had experienced over forty years ago. Yep, that's right. I had been feeling unforgiveness toward my mother, who gave me up for adoption when I was a baby. When I began to realize, it shocked me. I really thought I had dealt with my feelings. Like my brother not going back to the store, I was good with what had been done. "It is what it is" was my outlook. I even tried to sound strong and unconcerned, justifying what she did. "Maybe she did what she felt was best for me" or "I don't know what she may have been dealing with, we're all dealing with something." My feigned strength was only masking the anger, pain, and frustration I felt, knowing regardless of what was going on with her, she threw me away. She had no regard for my life and discarded me like yesterday's trash. She left me to die. She left me alone and unwanted, feeling abandoned and rejected. See? Another thing about going from pain to purpose is you must acknowledge your feelings. Be honest with yourself. Whatever was going on in her life, she took no care to ensure I had a chance. But as Joseph said in Gen 50:20, "As for you, you meant evil against me, but God meant it for good..." He helped me see because I don't know the details behind the reason she left me, I cannot always attribute it to the ideal of her not wanting me, but I can attribute it to the spirit of abandonment. You see? We must stop looking at people and blaming their flesh for their actions. If we are not careful, spirits will attach themselves to us and have us acting and doing things that aren't Christlike. As I was writing, those thoughts flooded my emotions, breaking forth like a dam, and before you know it, the spirit of unforgiveness became more prevalent than ever.

Being told no isn't just about God saying you can't have something. Being told no can sometimes be a set up for better. How can I say that? I started asking God why. Why would He allow me to endure all of that? My mother's actions had planted seeds of abandonment, pain, rejection, and insecurity. She hurt me, and all these years, I tried to make excuses for her, and even though I don't know for sure why, I knew enough to know, I was still hurt and yes, angry. I had been asking God for years to allow me to find information about my birth family. I began the search, and what I found was limited, but I persisted. There are things I want to do, questions I need answers to, places I want to go, but I've learned it's important we stop looking to others for an apology or validation. There's nothing wrong with wanting answers, but it's important that we allow God to be God. Isaiah 55:8-9 tells us, "For my thoughts are not your thoughts, neither are your ways my ways, saith the Lord. For as the heavens are higher than the earth, so are my ways higher than your ways, and my thoughts than your thoughts." Yes, there are some things you are better off, not knowing. Sometimes, knowing will cause more harm than good.

Being adopted, with no connection to my birth family, often made me feel alone and disconnected. Every time it seemed as though I was getting the information I needed, something would come up and stop me. I would think of another avenue to try, and something would stop me. I finally got some information, and upon reading it, I found myself licking my wounds once again. I didn't get the information I was looking for, finding out before I was adopted, I was in foster care, and after being in foster care for a while, the family decided they didn't want me and gave me back to the adoption agency. I became that little girl again, wanting to experience the joy of something and being told again, "No, you can't have that." Why didn't they want me?

If you're not careful, the enemy uses every little entrance he can to come in and have you spiraling. I was learning there are some things in life I will ever know. I may never know my birth family. I may never know if there's anyone else in this world with my DNA, besides my children and grandchildren. I must forgive. I will admit, even after finding that out, I kept digging. I guess you say I don't learn, do I? Well, I took what I knew and sought out official help. Again, the answer was no.

Now, you may be asking at this point, how does God fit into all of this, and what does this have to do with Him saying no? Sometimes, God won't allow certain things to be because He wants to show us Him. Eventually, I was adopted by the parents I call "Mom and

Dad." Life was good by some standards, but there were still some painful experiences. I experienced physical, verbal, and emotional abuse and was sexually molested. I have suffered mental breakdowns, was a widow by age twenty-three with three small children, and have experienced a devastatingly painful divorce. You know what God said? He directed me to Romans 8:28. "All things work together for good for those who love the Lord and are called according to His purpose." But all those things by themselves did not produce the desired outcome that God had for my life. It took every single situation to come together as a culmination of events to get to the place God wanted me to get to. All those things worked together. And though they may have been painful events, they all worked for my good. Things worked out.

I didn't know when I was young, I was called to His purpose. I only knew I hurt. He assured me every painful thing I had experienced worked out for my good, better than anything I would have experienced had my mother kept me. How could that be? How could my life be better without my mother? He reminded me I have never been without my mother. She is with me every single day in some shape or form. I don't know her, but I have her mannerisms, resemble her physically, and have some of her temperament. I also carry tendencies that are not so positive, and because of the actions of her and my father, I carried with me generational curses. One of the hardest things to fight and deal with are things you cannot see. How do I know? I came from her, and she will never stop being a part of me.

What I realized in all this process is never, ever, ever in all my life did I have any issues with the fact my father was not in the picture, either. For some reason, I found it easier to dismiss my father not being in my life. I never expressed any ill feelings toward him and never questioned why. I never sought out to know him, only my mother. God revealed to me, I had replaced my father in my mind with my adoptive father because he showed me more affection, which is what I needed. I looked at my adoptive mother and saw my biological mother. My adoptive mother was not very affectionate, so I equated that to the lack of love I felt, being rejected by my biological mother. I am working through the forgiveness process. I had to ask God for forgiveness for harboring those feelings and forgive myself for the way I saw my biological mother. I must also forgive my biological mother because I need to be free. What's crazy is she may never know I was upset with her. She may not even know I was still alive. She may not have even cared. Obviously, I don't know if she's still alive, but either way, I have to forgive because I need God to forgive me.

Unforgiveness stifles your prayer requests, and He says in his Word if we fail to forgive others, he will not forgive us. I must not only say it, I must let it become a part of me that I forgive her. There is so much more God wants me to do, and I'm going to need Him to help me do it. The last thing I need is for my prayers to be stifled because I am carrying around unforgiveness for her and others. Yep, there are some other people that I must forgive. Some I must forgive for hurting me and not wanting to realize they've hurt me. Some I must simply forgive because it's the right thing to do, and God said to do it. Even if you feel wronged but may not have been wronged, forgive. Even if you think there is something there that doesn't feel quite right, forgive. There will be times when we will ask God to do things in our life He will not do because we have not yet passed the test.

When I was in school, if we didn't get satisfactory grades at the end of the year, we weren't passed onto the next grade. Even though I've seen it done to students, passing them without them acquiring the necessary knowledge to proceed on causes an inability to effectively produce quality outcomes in life situations. It causes them, once again, to be unable to handle being told "no." There is no way to cross your bridge successfully without going through a process. We must cross plank by plank, step by step. If God allows us to just jump from situation to situation without passing the tests and fulfilling the requirements, we would be inadequately prepared, which would cause even more problems in the end.

Our inability to forgive causes us to harbor feelings of anger, resentment, frustration, judgment, and stagnation. Those spirits begin to eat at us, and before we know it, we are operating purely out of self, and there is no room for God to work in us.

Often, God will say no because he wants us to be properly prepared and equipped. He knows when we are not properly equipped, we are vulnerable in our battle against the enemy. "For we wrestle not against flesh and blood, but against principalities, against powers, gainst the rulers of the darkness of this world, against spiritual ickedness in high places." Eph 6:12 (NLT) Harboring those feelings akes us spiritually weak. We become so focused on the pain and he problem, we can't focus on the pain reliever and problem solver.

Iow do you know if you need to forgive someone? It's a personal nd individual assessment. Sometimes, just as a precaution, I will sk God to help me forgive anyone who has wronged me, or I *feel* as wronged me. There's no cookie-cutter procedure. How long oes it take to know you've forgiven someone? There's no definite nswer for that either. You'll know you're getting better when you ave a sense of peace about that person and the situation.

Allowing God to heal whatever is wrong is the key to forgiveness. t's not something you can do. I want to say that again—forgiveness s not something you can do. It is something you can participate in. To forgive, you must become a willing vessel of God. He is the only one who can remove the pain and dirt of unforgiveness and replace t with His love and peace. God does the work. He changes your heart and your mind. To be in that place also means you must place yourself within proximity of His presence to hear what He has to say and do what He tells you to do. The only way you can pass the test s to get quiet and listen to the instructor.

Perhaps your unforgiveness is not about a person who you feel wronged you? We know the importance of forgiveness, but during our issues and displeasure, has there ever been a time when we have questioned God and His sovereignty? Did we disagree with a decision he made and expressed that? Did we tell him there was no way what was going on could be for our good? Okay, well, maybe that's just me. Maybe I'm the only one who felt as if they had drawn the short end of the stick, and God needed to know how unfair it was. Perhaps I'm the only one who thought I should catch a break this time.

Even if I am the only one who will be honest enough to say they dealt with those feelings, I'm not the only one who has gone through it. I'm reminded about the story of Job, who endured pain, suffering, loss, and devastation, all at the behest of God. Others in the Bible sought God and needed him, but they were not always happy with the results. They questioned God and his presence in their lives. The Israelites complained and cried out to him about what he allowed to happen in their lives. Each scenario was God showing and telling them to "Turn back to me, be obedient, follow me, listen to me, serve me, worship me, TRUST ME."

I was driving one day and came to a bridge. I've told you I don't like bridges, especially high ones. Well, this bridge, in my opinion, was a high one. I began driving over it slowly and carefully. While driving across the bridge, God said this to me, "When you're crossing a bridge, it's important you maintain your lane. If not, you run the risk of running into someone else's lane and causing them harm. Go at your own pace. No one says you must cross this bridge in record time. Take your time. And lastly, just as you crossed this bridge, you trusted the bridge was intact, with no pieces missing. You trusted the beams were sturdy and present. You trusted this bridge to get you from where you were to where you want to go. Now, that's the way I want you to trust me. Trust that I am present and sturdy. There is nothing missing in me, and I will get you where you need to go, in the timeframe you need to be there, safe and sound."

When things happen to us, God is telling us the same thing, but what happens when you've prayed, and things still didn't go your way? Can you still say you didn't get angry with God? Perhaps you are dealing or have dealt with a situation that made you angry with God. Perhaps you feel he didn't allow you to get the job you wanted, or the relationship you wanted didn't work out. Perhaps your loved one was sick, and you prayed they would be healed, but they died anyway.

When my dad died, I was angry. Angry with myself because I felt like I hadn't done enough for him and angry because had I stayed in his hospital room with him just a little while longer, I would've been there when he had his heart attack. I was angry at people—people who I thought should've done more. I was angry with God because he seemed like he never answered my prayers. How could he take the one person in the world who loved me unconditionally? How could he take him when he had done so much good for others, yet leave other people who were vicious and mean? Why?

After that, I didn't want to pray or go to church. I didn't want to hear about God's love, but as I said, troubles will either push you toward God or away from God. As much as I was hurting and angry, emotions everywhere, I came to realize even in my worst moments with God, I was better off than my worst moments without Him. God knows we won't always understand. He knows we won't always agree, and that we're not going to like it, and yes, he knows sometimes, we'll lash out at him or walk away from him. But when it's all said and done, he is still saying, "I love you, I got you, just trust me." When I finally got to the point, I knew I needed God more than he needed me, I had to ask God to forgive me. Why? I made a false claim about God. I claimed he didn't care. I claimed he wasn't listening to my prayers. I claimed I didn't need him. I was wrong, extremely wrong. I had to go to him, humble myself before him, and ask for forgiveness. It wasn't a long, drawn-out dissertation or speech. That wasn't necessary. I went to my Daddy, my heavenly Father, and I said, "I'm sorry, God. I repent. Please forgive me." And guess what? I was forgiven. It's not always easy to recognize you're wrong because pride doesn't want us to be free. The Word tells us, "Where the spirit of the Lord is, there is liberty." So, no matter what you've done or how angry you've become with God, he is so loving, compassionate, gracious, merciful, and sovereign, all you have to do is come back and say, "God, please forgive me. I was wrong. I repent. I want to do what you want me to do. I want you to change me. I want you to help me. I want you to be in control and lead me. Forgive me, Father." Then ask God to help you to forgive yourself.

We are sometimes quick to forgive others and sometimes, just as quick to ask God to forgive us. We accept His forgiveness with glad hearts, but then turn around and look at ourselves with scorn and disdain. We say we accept Jesus Christ and His love, yet we harm ourselves and walk around with low self-esteem because we haven't yet forgiven ourselves. We walk around a shell of a person. We put on a façade and smile. We sing in church, pray, and shout. We speak in tongues and proclaim the gospel. We tell others about the goodness of God, yet we don't apply the forgiveness of God to ourselves. We speak in defeated tones and say, "I feel like God is able to do any and everything for others, but for me, I don't feel like He will." We can't seem to forgive ourselves for what we've done, but God has forgiven you, so you have permission to forgive yourself. What you've done might have been treacherous or trifling—maybe you were unfaithful or committed murder, maybe you lied or stolen. Whatever the case, there is nothing God will not forgive you for if you would allow Him, but to fully walk in your freedom, you must forgive yourself. To not forgive yourself will cause you to walk in a state of condemnation, and if we believe part of the Bible, we must believe all the Bible. Romans 8:1 tells us, "There is now, therefore, no condemnation for those who are in Christ Jesus." If you have faith to believe you are forgiven by him, you must know and believe, walk in, and live out the fact you do not have to live a condemned life. If God will cast our sins in the sea of forgiveness to be remembered no more, then we, too, should remember how to have short-term memory, then live, move, and have our being in Christ Jesus. Like a parent who shows unconditional love, God's love is even more so. He will welcome you back into his presence and restore you unto him. He won't condemn you or scold you. He won't ridicule you or make fun of you. He will take you, love on you, and restore you unto Him, all the while healing your hurt. I read this in a devotion once, "If we are willing to meet Jesus in the places where we were wounded the deepest, we can see God perform His greatest miracles."

Reflections

Matthew 6:14

For if you forgive others their trespasses, your Heavenly Father will forgive you.

Proverbs 28:13

Whoever conceals his transgressions will not prosper.

Psalm 86:5

For you, O Lord, are good and forgiving, abounding in steadfast love to all who call upon you.

Micah 7:18

Who is a God like you, pardoning iniquity and passing over transgression?

2 Chronicles 30:9

For the Lord your God is gracious and merciful and will not turn away His face from you if you return to Him.

Write It Down

The "F" Word

The "F" word is one of the hardest words to say. What I want you to do in this section is think of people, things, and situations that still cause you pain, anger, or emotions and write them down. Then write what you feel happened to you that caused those feelings. Remember, this is just for you and God. He understands. Express what you're upset about, then I want you to say this. "God, help me to forgive." Repeat this as much as you need, as often as you need, and every time you think of something else, write it here. Then write it in your section for prayers. Now watch God work.

Chapter 8

DON'T GIVE UP, START SINGING

"For if I pray in a tongue, my spirit prays but my mind is unfruitful. What am I to do? I will pray with my spirit, but I will pray with my mind also; I will sing praise with my spirit, but I will sing with my mind also." 1 Cor. 14:14–15.

Different things appeal to different people. For instance, some people eat when they become stressed or upset, some people don't eat. I am one of those people. Both ends of the spectrum aren't healthy, but I often find I don't have an appetite. We also may have other coping mechanisms. For me, music is a soother. It speaks to me in ways other things can't. I love music—listening to it, singing it, writing it. I love various genres. It's an easy release for me, what I use to take me to another place. As I'm writing this to you, I am playing my praise and worship music. I'm not in a stressful place, but I find the music speaks to my spirit and puts me in a place of calmness and peace. Some people often say, "I can't sing, so I don't even try." I've found it's not about the sound you make but about the heart in the song you sing. Other people may use exercise to take them to that place of serenity or peace, others may use reading. We all have a way of dealing with what we're facing. When we can cope and deal with what we're facing, it has a way of affecting everything around us. When you are on this journey, you will need to have something positive to focus on. Like when women give birth, they are told to look and focus on something that calms them to take their mind off the pain. If we find Christ and focus on Him, He will help us to navigate and cross this bridge safely and with purpose.

While music may not be your thing, it's mine, and I want to share a story with you about singing that helps me. Acts 16 verses 16-26 tells about Paul and Silas, who had been ministering and were arrested for casting the demon out of a young girl, who was a soothsayer or fortune teller. They found themselves in a dark situation like ones we find ourselves in. They were cast aside, beaten, locked up, and punished for what God had told them to do. Much like when you give your best on the job, and you're still passed up for the promotion, when you have been faithful in your relationship and still abandoned, or going to church and praying all the time, and your loved one still died. They were arrested and thrown in prison for doing exactly what God had called them to do, for doing what they thought was the right thing, yet God still allowed them to experience issues.

While in prison, they had every reason to moan and groan. They could've argued, complained, and given up. They could have lamented over the fact they were doing the right thing but ended up in jail. They could've laid there and "licked their wounds." They could have said, "Oh, woe is me," but instead, they began to sing songs of praise and give thanks. They began to find the good in their situation. What was good in their situation? God, life, and the fact they were still alive. The scripture doesn't say they faced death, but in those days, the disciples and other followers of Christ did, so you can imagine facing death was probably something they thought about.

Every day we face death, not so much physical death, even though that's a realization, but the death of our dreams, aspirations, goals, promises, and destinies. We face the possibility if we give up, if we give in, if we throw in the towel, we will die. Even though we face the possibility of those things dying, we can still find the good in it. Every day we wake up, we are blessed with the opportunity to try again, to make those dreams a reality. We have the chance to make a difference in our lives and the lives of others.

We must remember our lives are not just one dimensional, we are not one-dimensional beings. All of us, like it or not, are connected to someone else, and how we deal with and respond to our situations affects other people, much like my brother and the ice cream. It's okay to be upset, throw temper tantrums, or pout because we don't get what we want or where we want in life, but I want to let you know there is someone who is waiting for you to start singing. What happens when you sing? Let's look at the story again. When Paul and Silas began to sing, there was a huge earthquake, the doors of the cells flew open, and each prisoner's chains fell off. Did you get that?! That excited me so much. Because of Paul and Silas' singing, others were set free.

Do you know there are those waiting to be set free, and no one else can do it but you? I know your prayer wasn't answered the way you thought, or the outcome wasn't exactly how you envisioned it, but even amid your pain and sorrow, there is someone who needs you, someone needs you to sing. Through your transparency and willingness to share, someone else will be delivered. Being in a place of praise takes the focus from your problems and puts it on Jesus, the Problem Solver. It takes the focus from your disappointment and places it on the one who can do exceedingly and abundantly above all that you would even be able to think or ask. You can't begin to imagine all the things God is waiting to do in your life. You can't afford to give up now. You have to keep singing.

Let me share this with you as well. You can't give up because the very next step may be what catapults you to your destiny. Yes, there may be some pieces missing in your bridge here and there, but you can't stop. Even if the step is missing, watch God fill it in. The next tep may seem shaky, but God will stabilize it. God said, "He knows he plans He has for you." Those plans don't always allow us a sneak eek, so we don't really know what's coming. Trusting God allows is to take one step at a time, believing He knows what's best. We an be confident it's going to be okay because He's already in the uture. Behind every disappointment, every failure, every obstacle, very heartbreak, every denial, behind every NO is a YES! There is YES, and it has your name on it.

'ou can't stop singing. Not once do you see in the Bible, a song, or a ıymn about any uncertainty on the part of God. Never do we read hat God was going bless us but changed his mind or that God vould withhold any good thing from us. Never do we hear that God urned away from us in our moments of need and desperation. Our lesh makes us feel that way, but our spirit lets us know there is no riend like Jesus, and there is no one that can do the things He does or us, with us, and to us. "With Him, all things are possible!"

Иy friend, your crossing from pain to purpose may feel ıncomfortable right now. You may even feel as though there is no vay you will make it. Trust me, I've been there, and I understand. I often sit and look back over my life and remember those times when thought I was literally going to die from the pain I felt in my heart. Many times, I have been riding along, and suddenly, it hits me, 'Wow, I'm still here!"

After my father passed, I didn't think I would be able to make it, iterally thought I would die. That was a pain I don't wish on anybody. One thing I've learned is problems and pain in life will cause you to either pull away from God or push you toward Him. To be honest, when my dad died, I pulled away from God. I didn't want to hear about God, didn't want to feel God, didn't want to seek God. Ever been there? However, I kept feeling this pull, this tug, this drawing in me. There were days when I could barely get up, days when depression set in so strongly, I didn't know if I was coming or going. Crossing the bridge from pain to purpose wasn't even in my mind. Some days, survival wasn't even in my mind. Some days, waking up wasn't in my mind. There have been days in my life, I didn't want to survive, but while crossing my bridges, I kept singing. What is interesting is I didn't even know I was singing. How is that?

There were some mornings I would subconsciously hear a song in my head. I like to say I had a song in my heart, but I didn't take notice of it all the time. Every now and then, it would just dawn on me, I woke up to a song. Those songs would replay over and over in my head. It's been over seven years since my dad passed, and guess what? I'm still singing. The songs are still in my head and my heart when I wake up. Some days, they linger, and some days, after I'm awake for a while, it subsides. It's not the melody that relieves me, but the words of the song. Some songs are praise and worship, some are contemporary, and then there are those that are old hymns I grew up singing in church.

Yes, there are scabs that are evidence of healing that still needs to be done. I still must deal with unpleasant reminders of decisions I've made. I still talk to God about why certain things didn't go my way and why He didn't allow some things to be, but I know He knows what's best for me. And even during those times when I don't want to "eat my vegetables," I thank God that every day, I have a chance to make a difference. Just as Paul and Silas sang praises and gave thanks, I sing and give thanks. That is my coping mechanism. I pray through my songs and prayers that others will be released and set free from whatever keeps them bound.

Don't give up my friends, start singing.

Reflections

1 Corinthians 14:14–15

In right worship: For if I pray in a tongue, my spirit prays but my mind is unfruitful. What am I to do? I will pray with my spirit, but I will pray with my mind also; I will sing praise with my spirit, but I will sing with my mind also.

Psalm 103:1-5 NASB

Bless the Lord, O my soul, and all that is within me, bless His holy name. Bless the Lord, O my soul, and forget none of His benefits; Who pardons all your iniquities, Who heals all your diseases; Who redeems your life from the pit, Who crowns you with lovingkindness and compassion. Who satisfies your years with good things, So that your youth is renewed like the eagle.

2 Corinthians 4:15

For it is all for your sake, so that as grace extends to more and more people, it may increase thanksgiving, to the glory of God.

Philippians 4:6-7

Do not be anxious about anything, but in everything by prayer and supplication with thanksgiving let your requests be made known to God.

And the peace of God, which surpasses all understanding, will guard your hearts and your minds in Christ Jesus.

Psalm 95:2

Let us come into his presence with thanksgiving; let us make a joyful noise to him with songs of praise!

1 Chronicles 16:34

Oh give thanks to the LORD, for he is good; for his steadfast love endures forever!

2 Corinthians 4:15

For it is all for your sake, so that as grace extends to more and more people it may increase thanksgiving, to the glory of God.

Write It Down

What's Important?

How important is it to you to know God has not left you? What ways can you find joy in your situation? How will you help someone else?

ABOUT THE AUTHOR

Insert your author profile information here. Insert your author profile information here. Insert your author profile information here. Insert your author profile information here.

Insert your author profile information here. Insert your author profile information here. Insert your author profile information here. Insert your author profile information here. Insert your author profile information here.

Insert your author profile information here. Insert your author profile information here. Insert your author profile information here. Insert your author profile information here. Insert your author profile information here.

Insert your author profile information here. Insert your author profile information here. Insert your author profile information here.

Insert your author profile information here. Insert your author profile information here.

Made in the USA
Middletown, DE
04 September 2024

59846705R00113